BRITISH PORCELAIN

SHIRE PUBLICATIONS LTD

BRITISH PORCELAIN

JOHN SANDON

SHIRE PUBLICATIONS LTD

Published in Great Britain in 2009 by Shire Publications Ltd,
Midland House, West Way, Botley, Oxford OX2 0PH, United
Kingdom.
443 Park Avenue South, New York, NY 10016, USA.

E-mail: shire@shirebooks.co.uk www.shirebooks.co.uk

A CIP catalogue record for this book is available from the
British Library.

Shire Collections no. 3   ·   ISBN-13: 978 0 74780 713 1

John Sandon has asserted his right under the Copyright,
Designs and Patents Act, 1988, to be identified as the author
of this book.

Designed by Ken Vail Graphic Design, Cambridge, UK and
typeset in Bembo.
Printed in China through Worldprint Ltd.

09 10 11 12 13   10 9 8 7 6 5 4 3 2 1

COVER IMAGE
A pair of Chelsea figures known as the 'Imperial Shepherds',
35 cm high, from the Gold Anchor period, c. 1765.

PAGE 2 IMAGE
A Flight, Barr and Barr Worcester vase of impressive size,
decorated with a rich 'Japan' pattern finished off with bright
gilding, 40cm high, c 1825.

ACKNOWLEDGEMENTS

In the great majority of cases, where no individual
acknowledgement is given, illustrations show pieces sold by
Bonhams. This book would not have been possible without
access to the precious archive of pieces that have passed
through my hands during thirty-three years as a specialist
at 101 New Bond Street, London W1.

CONTENTS

Chapter One

ALCHEMY AND INVENTION: 1740–55

IN 2008 a new discovery shocked the world of antique ceramics. Archive evidence was published suggesting that the Duke of Buckingham made the first English porcelain in the 1670s, during the reign of Charles II. To put this in perspective, it looks likely that porcelain was made in England before any of the great French factories like St Cloud or Chantilly. It was made a full forty years before the discovery of porcelain at Meissen in Germany. So far just four priceless specimens of the Duke of Buckingham's porcelain are known to survive, three of them at Burghley House in Lincolnshire where they were listed in an inventory in 1688. Little is known about the Duke's porcelain-making venture and we are not certain where his little painted and gilded vases were made. Production must have been on a very small scale and so new examples are unlikely to turn up unrecognised in any collection. It is, however, exciting to think that apart from the legendary 'Medici porcelain' created in Renaissance Italy, porcelain was probably made in England before anywhere else in Europe.

We have to jump forward to the 1740s before the next successful porcelain was made in England, but this does not mean that there was no porcelain in use in Britain. Far from it, in fact, for the trade in fine porcelain was big business. Porcelain imports from China expanded at an incredible rate to feed an insatiable demand in Europe. Royalty, the nobility and wealthy merchants all wanted to dine off precious white porcelain, while fine ladies and gentlemen could not stand high in society unless they served their friends tea in fashionable china cups.

Recent excavations in the East End of London have revealed the extent of the international china business in the seventeenth century. Bowls and dishes of Chinese Ming porcelain were used in the homes of the privateers whose pirate vessels travelled the world capturing and trading in precious cargoes. By the time of Queen Anne, special designs created for English tables were brought from the Orient and sold for huge prices at auctions in London. Some were special orders decorated with coats of arms of wealthy English families, the patterns sent to China to be copied and returned as complete services. Early in the eighteenth century a new trade of china painter is noted in London records. For customers who didn't want to wait up to two years for their order to arrive from China, special designs and armorial bearings were now painted onto plain Chinese porcelain in decorating workshops in London. Early English enamelling on Chinese 'blanks' was a bigger business than previously thought, but even so, British output hardly registers alongside the vast and valuable trade in imported oriental porcelain.

To most people in England, Chinese porcelain was as mysterious as the place from which it came. Oriental goods were brought back by the 'East India

This Chinese porcelain chocolate pot was shipped from China in plain white and then enamelled in England, 12.2 cm high, c. 1700–20. The figure painting was inspired by early travel books such as Nieuhof's Embassy to China, *published in 1665.*

Company', often by way of India, and there was natural confusion as to its origin. A common description used in England for Chinese imported porcelain in the eighteenth century was 'India China Ware'. The same ships brought to Europe mixed cargoes of Chinese and Japanese porcelain, but customers did not care where it was from, they just wanted as much as they could get.

The factories at Jingdezhen in China were designed for mass production and a relatively small number of different patterns were made in enormous quantities, to be assembled into sets when they reached European china dealers. In recent years a great deal has been learnt about the china trade from a series of shipwrecks recovered from the seas of Asia where the vessels foundered en route to Europe. In 1985 Captain Michael Hatcher discovered the wreck of the *Geldermalsen*, a Dutch East Indiaman that set sail from Canton in January 1752 destined for Europe with nearly a quarter of a million pieces of Chinese porcelain on board. While in some years the loss of such a cargo would have caused a severe shortage of porcelain in Europe, in the mid eighteenth century some fifteen times this amount was shipped annually, enough to allow for the occasional maritime disaster. In 1986 150,000 pieces recovered from the *Geldermalsen* were auctioned in Amsterdam as the 'Nanking Cargo', generating enormous publicity and high prices for what was in fact quite ordinary Chinese porcelain.

Had the ship not sunk in 1752, this porcelain would have been sold all over Europe, generating massive profits for the businessmen who had invested in the cargo. Huge profits were made from the oriental porcelain trade and as a result there was no shortage of English entrepreneurs who dreamt of sharing these profits by making their own porcelain. The problem was the lack of know-how and the correct materials to create porcelain in England.

Initially, copies of Chinese porcelain were made using pottery. Plates and dishes of English delftware looked for all the world like porcelain from China, but they were made of earthenware covered with an opaque white glaze. Unlike Chinese porcelain, delft was not translucent – you can't see light through pottery – and when the soft glaze chipped off the rims, the true nature of the coarse clay body was revealed underneath. Even so, for more than a century delftware was the best substitute for porcelain Britain could come up with.

John Dwight was a contemporary of the Duke of Buckingham. At his pottery in Fulham Dwight experimented with porcelain manufacture but failed to perfect his firing methods. Instead, in the late 1600s Dwight was a successful manufacturer of a kind of high-fired pottery called saltglazed stoneware. During the eighteenth century potters in Staffordshire perfected this stoneware and some of this was enamelled in colours to resemble Chinese porcelain. By the 1740s some beautifully thin saltglazed stoneware was made in Staffordshire, but it was creamy in colour – not white – and you can't see light through it.

Chinese porcelain plates from the 'Nanking Cargo', recovered from the wreck of the Geldermalsen, *sunk on its way to Europe in 1752. 22 cm diameter.*

The quest for porcelain in Britain became a serious matter. Several foreigners arrived in England claiming knowledge of secret processes and seeking wealthy backers, but most were charlatans who lacked the right raw materials, especially kaolin. Successful china factories were now operating in Germany and France, backed by kings and princes. In England the government and the King showed little interest, however, and refused to invest in a state porcelain manufactory. In Britain it was left to private entrepreneurs to establish china factories, and they needed chemists who could create the right kind of clay and construct suitable kilns.

Thomas Briand was invited to address the Royal Society in 1742, so his claims to have invented porcelain were at least taken seriously. Briand may have came from France and the porcelain he developed was probably a soft paste 'Frit' porcelain but not as creamy as the French *pâte tendre*. Thomas Briand settled in Staffordshire, but it is not known if his china making was successful as no pieces have been identified. Nicholas Sprimont, the proprietor of the Chelsea factory is usually credited with inventing Chelsea porcelain, but his contribution was probably more artistic than scientific. He may have learnt about frit porcelain from an associate of Briand's. As a silversmith, Sprimont had his finger on the pulse of the latest fashion and was friends with all the right people including the artist Hogarth, the sculptor Roubiliac and wealthy businessman Sir Everard Faulkener who provided finance. The Chelsea porcelain factory opened on a high note, probably in 1744.

The first phase of the factory, from around 1745 to 1749, is known as the 'Triangle Period' after the factory mark of a triangle that was incised into the paste. Within a few months Chelsea's porcelain body and glaze had already passed the experimental stage and in its earliest years the factory made a highly-translucent white porcelain, evenly fired and thinly cast.

A pair of Chelsea table salts adorned with crayfish, 11–12 cm wide, from the Triangle period, c. 1745–8. These perfectly capture the spirit of rococo.

A Limehouse teapot decorated in the style of old Japanese porcelain, the enamelling probably added by an independent china painter working in London, 12.6 cm high, c. 1746–8.

When studying English porcelain it is important to appreciate the kind of market at which each factory was aimed. Chelsea saw no reason to compete with imported Chinese porcelain and instead was influenced by English silver which, as a silversmith, Nicholas Sprimont knew so well. Coffee pots and beakers moulded with plants were left undecorated or just partly coloured in bright enamels to emphasise the beautiful white glaze. The spirit of rococo was superbly captured by shell salts adorned with crayfish and jugs modelled with goats and a bee delicately alighting on the side.

During Chelsea's Triangle period, another London factory came and went. At Limehouse, in the East End, Joseph Wilson and Co. produced porcelain for no more than three years between 1746 and 1748. The lively shapes of Limehouse sauceboats show the influence of English silver, while in contrast the decoration, almost entirely painted in underglaze blue, copied Chinese imports of the time. In the end this proved to be Limehouse's failing, for the control of their glaze was poor, resulting in cloudiness and black firespecks. Customers used to the smooth, clear glaze on imported Chinese tearwares expected better, and in 1748 the Limehouse manufactory closed. Limehouse was only identified in 1989 when a carefully planned excavation dug up unfinished fragments on the site of the factory, and these matched a type of porcelain previously ascribed to Liverpool. Limehouse porcelain is rare today and because of its early date it is exciting and valuable too.

Following the failure of the Limehouse factory, at least one potter who had worked there went to Bristol where, from 1749, Benjamin Lund's small factory made porcelain in a closely related style. Lund's Bristol factory continued to make silver-shaped sauceboats with Chinese decoration in blue. The Bristol porcelain was much whiter in appearance than Limehouse had been, but the glaze was still heavy and blurring of the decoration generally spoilt the intended effect. This early Bristol porcelain factory lasted less than two years.

A Lund's Bristol sauceboat, the shape copying English silver, 23.8 cm long, c. 1749–50. A visitor to the Bristol factory described white sauceboats for sale at 16s a pair, a very high price at the time.

Another factory in East London succeeded where Limehouse failed. The date of the earliest Bow porcelain is uncertain and research is very much ongoing. Possibly following a long period of experimentation, Thomas Frye, a gifted portrait painter, and Edward Heylyn took out a patent in 1744 for a new kind of English porcelain. A further patent for a different kind of porcelain was taken out by Frye alone in 1749. The earliest porcelain attributed with certainty to Bow during the 1740s comprises teawares, mugs and pickle dishes with a mushroom-grey tint to the body and very bright *famille rose* enamelling copied from Chinese imports. Other pieces were painted in underglaze blue.

RIGHT
An early Bow teapot with famille rose *decoration, 14.2 cm high, c. 1746–8. The earliest Bow porcelain is described as having a mushroom-grey tint.*

OPPOSITE BOTTOM
A Worcester cream jug painted with a 'Long Eliza' figure, 8.4 cm high, c. 1753–4. While the shape is derived from silver, the decoration is essentially Chinese although with a Worcester twist.

The date 1750 appears on a series of inkwells inscribed 'Made at New Canton'. These show that Bow's porcelain had changed slightly by this date and was now much whiter in appearance. While not as fine as Chelsea, Bow made porcelain cheaply and in quantity. The factory buildings were modelled on the architecture of the East India Company's warehouse in Canton and by calling his works 'New Canton' it is clear where Frye's and his partners' ambitions lay. At Bow direct imitations were made of Chinese blue and white, plain white porcelain known as '*blanc de chine*' and enamelled decoration in the celebrated *famille rose* palette. Bow also copied Japanese 'Imari' wares painted in red, blue and gold. Alongside these, the Bow factory made shapes that were not available from the Orient, such as sauceboats, shell pickle stands and handles for cutlery. Bow's porcelain formula was 'phosphatic' which means that it contained burnt animal bone. This gave Bow porcelain stability and the material was well suited for making plates and dishes. These sold well, and the Bow factory grew to a large size.

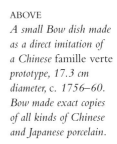

ABOVE
A small Bow dish made as a direct imitation of a Chinese famille verte *prototype, 17.3 cm diameter, c. 1756–60. Bow made exact copies of all kinds of Chinese and Japanese porcelain.*

The Worcester Porcelain manufactory was established in 1751 by fifteen businessmen who put up capital to exploit a porcelain recipe invented by a local doctor, John Wall and his friend William Davis. Their experiments, apparently using an iron cauldron in the back of Davis's apothecary shop, can certainly be likened to alchemy, and their amateur attempts to copy Chinese blue and white plates in a new factory failed. To save their investment, the Worcester partners combined their experiences with Benjamin Lund's Bristol operation, and by changing the firing methods they succeeded in perfecting 'steatitic' porcelain. This was made from a special ingredient known as 'soaprock' mined in Cornwall. Worcester soon learned how to control their blue and white to prevent blurring, and they also made wares that were beautifully enamelled. Worcester knew that customers in England wanted Chinese designs, but saw little point in merely imitating the Orient as Bow had done. Instead artists at Worcester created their own style, using English silver shapes and a new kind of painting that was loosely derived from Meissen's *chinoiserie*. Worcester's speciality was teaware, for their 'steatitic' formula was incredibly durable. It produced teapots that could withstand boiling water without cracking, a fault that plagued every other English maker. Customers flocked to buy Worcester's teapots and delicate coffee cups.

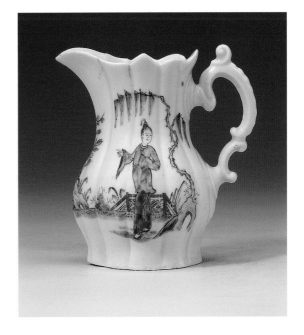

ABOVE
*A Derby figure of a map
seller, from the Planché
period, 15 cm high,
c. 1750–5. These very
early Derby figures can be
exciting, especially when
left in the white.*

ABOVE RIGHT
A Longton Hall jug with
chinoiserie *decoration,
20.5 cm high, c. 1755–
6. This curious cruciform
jug is one of many shapes
unique to this
Staffordshire factory.*

Two other factories outside London came to prominence during the early 1750s.
Derby porcelain was disadvantaged by its inability to stand up to heat during use
and instead of making teawares Derby initially made mostly figurines. Andrew
Planché had been involved with ceramic experiments since the 1730s and he
possibly assisted Briand and Sprimont at Chelsea. Planché commenced the
manufacture of figures at Derby around 1750. His early figures can be exciting,
especially when left in the white, for the modelling was of a high standard and
original, unlike the direct copies of Meissen favoured by other English factories.
William Duesbury, a London enameller and china dealer, came to Derby in 1756
to take control of the factory. Teawares were still avoided because of the instability
of the paste, but the Meissen influence is seen in baskets, leaf dishes and rococo
vases, which became a speciality. Figure production continued with maintained
standards of modelling and decoration.

In Staffordshire at Longton Hall, William Littler's porcelain was very individual,
combining Chelsea and Meissen styles with rustic pottery. His early production,
from 1750–2, was quite primitive but once Littler overcame firing difficulties, his
porcelain became exciting. Leaf shapes of all sorts, cabbages, cauliflowers and
strawberries were painted in bright, lurid colours combined with naive landscapes
and bird painting. A particularly bright underglaze blue, used as a ground colour, is
known as 'Littler's Blue', a distinctive if perhaps overpowering speciality of the

factory in its later years. Longton Hall figures lack the quality of Chelsea or Derby examples, but they have much to commend them, partly because they are so individual. The earliest specimens are known as 'snowmen' figures, an appropriate name as the thick, opaque white glaze hides any finely modelled detail.

During the first decade of English porcelain, there were other porcelain makers in England, not all of which are fully understood. Distinctive groups of porcelains have been linked together by appearance, glaze, colour and design and new research is gradually putting names to these different groups. Nicholas Crisp and John Sanders made steatitic porcelain at Vauxhall in London between 1751 and 1763, but this was only recognised in 1988 when a group of wares, previously thought to have been Liverpool,

ABOVE
A Derby basket for a dessert of fruit, 21.5 cm wide, c. 1760. Lively fruit painting was a speciality of Derby at this time and cherries were particularly favoured.

LEFT
A Longton Hall figure representing Winter, 13.3 cm high, c. 1750–2. When left in the white, the earliest Longton Hall models are appropriately known as 'snowmen' figures. This example has, typically, collapsed during the kiln firing and leans to one side.

was matched with fragments excavated at Vauxhall. Crisp's porcelain largely copied Chinese designs, but European flower decoration and experimental colour printing was also attempted.

Liverpool is something of a minefield for porcelain collectors and researchers. Many china factories were based there producing very similar wares, and much has been incorrectly attributed in the past. During the 1750s Samuel Gilbody, Richard Chaffers and William Reid ran separate factories making porcelain in Liverpool, much of it directly copying either Worcester or Chinese prototypes. Workmen undoubtedly moved from one maker to another, adding to the confusion 250 years later.

Two very important, early English porcelain makers have caused even more confusion than all the others. Research has now identified one of these. The 'Girl in a Swing' factory baffled collectors for a century by its similarity to Chelsea. We now know that St James's was the location of this factory, established in about 1749 by Charles Gouyn, a jeweller who understood the market in expensive trinkets. His small factory in London made 'toys' – porcelain seals, scent bottles, snuff boxes and other novelties, as well as a number of distinctive larger figures and animals. These figures include the famous model of a girl in a swing, which gave the short-lived factory its popular collectors' name.

RIGHT
A Vauxhall tea canister decorated with European flowers, 11 cm high, c. 1755–6. This decoration uses an experimental process known as polychrome printing, used only at Vauxhall.

BELOW
A St James's porcelain scent bottle, 9.4 cm high, c. 1752–5. Charles Gouyn's small factory specialised in these delightful 'toys'.

The jury is still undecided on the other mystery factory. A few dozen pieces of English porcelain of exceptional quality survive from the mid 1740s. These include some pieces marked with the letter 'A' painted or scratched on the base, and so this has become known as 'A-mark porcelain'. Chemical analysis shows it to be similar to the porcelain recipe patented in 1744 by Frye and Heylyn and if this is the case it was made in East London at Stratford, close to Bow. The decoration of A-mark porcelain links indirectly to some of the earliest painting found both on Triangle-period Chelsea and early Bow. This suggests A-mark porcelain was made in London and tends to rule out another school of thought that favours a Scottish origin. Experimental porcelain was believed to have been made around 1750 just south of Edinburgh by Alexander Lind under the patronage of the Duke of Argyll.

It took many decades of speculation and research before Limehouse and Vauxhall porcelains were finally identified. Some day we hope a key piece of the research jigsaw will slot into place and we will know for sure where the A-mark porcelain was really made. That will still leave Greenwich and Stourbridge and Birmingham porcelain to be identified. Collectors actually like mysteries and a bit of intrigue keeps people interested.

A coffee cup of 'A-mark porcelain', believed to have been made in London in the 1740s, 6 cm high.

Chapter Two

BLUE AND WHITE PORCELAIN: 1748–90

WHEN most people think of Chinese porcelain, they envisage blue and white. This great Chinese invention goes back to the Yuan dynasty in the thirteenth century. During the Ming dynasty that followed, a few treasured specimens of blue Chinese porcelain gradually arrived in medieval Europe via Middle Eastern trade routes. In Britain the courts of Henry VIII and Elizabeth I proudly displayed blue and white Chinese bowls mounted in costly silver. Ming dishes were placed in the still life paintings of seventeenth-century Dutch 'Old Masters', for blue and white represented wealth. Three hundred years ago, European collectors of blue and white were fanatical. 'China Rooms' were all the rage and no self-respecting palace was without one. This meant, literally, wall-to-wall Chinese porcelain. The stunning effect of blue and white crowded together on a wall or in an alcove was the very height of fashion. If it was good enough for Queen Mary, or the King of Saxony, then every ambitious nobleman had to have a China Room too. Chinese blue and white porcelain was consequently expensive and it is little wonder it was copied in Europe.

The typical seventeenth-century Chinese export ware, known as *kraak* porcelain, was not particularly fine, but the Chinese had no desire to sell their best ware to foreigners. The trading companies wanted to make bigger profits anyway, by paying as little as they could for the porcelain in Canton. During the turmoil that followed the overthrow of the Ming Dynasty, the porcelain kilns at Jingdezhen were largely destroyed, creating a shortage of blue and white available in the West. Later in the seventeenth century, with Imperial control restored, the Chinese factories began to make fine porcelain once more for the Emperor and his court and some of this was sold for export. During the reign of the Emperor Kangxi (1662–1722) much wonderful porcelain arrived in the West. This appealed to collectors and was generally used for display rather than for making tea.

During the reigns of Yongzheng (1723–35) and Qianlong (1735–95) the quality of Chinese blue and white did not really decline but somehow pieces lacked the special excitement of Kangxi blue and white. The intricate painting was replaced by more robust shading and uneven washes of blue. The principal designs remained precise and clear and the potting was competent but not as delicate as before. Serving dishes were heavier and practical. The lids of tureens fitted perfectly and, in a service every piece matched the next with an exactness most modern manufacturers would be proud of. The mechanical nature of the painting is consistent with the image of rows and rows of Chinese blue painters passing plates along their bench, each adding their own part of the pattern. The unbelievable precision of the hand painting leaves you breathless, and still these were shipped to

OPPOSITE
A Lowestoft mug painted with a bathing hut on the local beach, inscribed 'A Trifle from Lowestoft' 14 cm high, c. 1785. Lowestoft does not get much more individual than this.

The author demonstrating the process of underglaze blue. Once glazed and fired, the black cobalt oxide on this vase will turn blue.

England and sold for affordable sums. In the 1740s and early 1750s, trading ships such as the *Geldermalsen* brought enormous quantities of Chinese porcelain to Europe (see pages 8–9) and still it all found a ready market.

The process of making blue and white is remarkably simple, involving a basic chemical reaction. Colours in ceramics are largely oxides of metals. The characteristic blue colour is created from cobalt oxide, which in nature is black rather than blue. A powder of finely crushed cobalt oxide is mixed with water or oil to make a paint suitable for decorating porcelain. This is painted directly onto the surface of unglazed porcelain. Glaze is largely made of silicon. When the porcelain is covered with glaze and placed in a kiln, the glass-like glaze melts over the surface. The cobalt oxide reacts with the silicon in the glaze, forming cobalt silicate, which is blue.

The result is therefore a pattern in blue, sealed indelibly beneath the protective layer of glaze. Underglaze blue is permanent. It never fades or flakes off. The biggest problem when making blue and white porcelain is preventing the blue decoration running or blurring as the melted glass flows over it.

Copying Chinese blue and white was a big business in Europe. Delftware, the principal type of pottery in Holland and in England, lacked the delicate translucency of porcelain, but for display delft plates served the purpose well. Cups and teapots were another matter, however and delft was totally unsuited for making tea. There is evidence that potters in England were experimenting with porcelain during the 1730s. Success had been achieved already in France and Germany but it was a costly business. The 'hard paste' formula used at Meissen was perfect for copying precious Japanese enamelled porcelain and for richly gilded decoration, but underglaze blue proved difficult to control. Meissen persisted but it wasn't until later in the eighteenth century that blue and white became an increasing part of Germany's porcelain production. The creamy soft paste porcelain of France was used for stunning blue and white early in the eighteenth century but it was always a costly luxury and could never compete with imported Chinese porcelain.

This was to be the main problem in Britain too. Once porcelain was discovered and factories became established during the 1740s, factory owners worked to perfect the production of blue and white. The problem once again was the price. Unless English porcelain could match the price of imported Chinese porcelain, it would struggle to be a profitable enterprise. As a silversmith, Nicholas Sprimont, the proprietor of the Chelsea porcelain factory, understood the market in luxury goods. He realised from the outset that his porcelain had to sell for a high price and so, apart from a handful of experiments and a very limited number of elegant blue patterns, Chelsea chose to ignore the whole area of blue and white.

Across the city in the East End of London it was a different story. It is a matter of argument as to which factory succeeded first, but both Bow and Limehouse were making blue and white by 1746. Their products generally went in different directions, however. The earliest Bow porcelain was strongly influenced by the Orient, both in form and decoration. Some shapes such as sauceboats and pickle dishes were uniquely British, but these were mostly decorated in the same way as Bow's plainer shapes, with direct copies of Chinese or Japanese porcelain patterns.

Compared with Chelsea, the 'new invented Limehouse ware' was a very different kind of porcelain. While Chelsea made porcelain for cabinets and for show, Limehouse ware was intended to be functional. With the best intentions, however, the Limehouse factory struggled from the outset. Basically it had trouble making plates and cups and saucers, the very shapes the Chinese did so well. The solution was to create shapes that customers in England wanted, but were not available from China. Due to problems moulding their sticky clay, the Chinese couldn't make very good oval objects, and they had trouble with embossed ornament. This gave Limehouse a chance. In Britain before the era of refrigeration, meat and fish were rarely served fresh and often tasted salty because the usual way to preserve meat was to cake it in salt. Strong sauces or spicy pickles were essential to disguise the stale or salty taste of the food.

A Limehouse pickle dish in the shape of a scallop shell, 11.4 cm wide, c. 1746–8. The Chinese emblems are copied from earlier Kangxi blue and white.

A pair of silver sauceboats placed on the dining table showed off its owners' wealth. Chinese porcelain was regarded as precious, too. By making an expensive sauceboat out of porcelain, Joseph Wilson must have believed everyone would want his Limehouse ware. English porcelain was new, however, and the British public were suspicious. Why would customers in London trust Limehouse ware? English pottery sauceboats were prone to crack when hot sauce was poured in. Chinese porcelain was tried and tested, so the remedy was obvious. If Limehouse sauceboats were painted like Chinese blue and white porcelain, success would be assured. Dishes for serving pickle did not need to withstand heat, but Limehouse pickle dishes were still painted with Chinese designs. Before Limehouse was available, most homes used real scallop shells to serve their pickles. Limehouse naturally responded by making their pickle dishes in the shape of shells or leaves. Large numbers were made.

If Limehouse ware was so innovative, why did the factory fail? Unfortunately, Limehouse wasn't good enough. Collectors love the humour of Limehouse – they find the details amusing. Sauceboats have feet moulded with lions' masks and these lions have silly grins. The chinamen painted on Limehouse are cartoon-like. In 1747, though, customers respected the precision of silver sauceboats and the clean, smooth glaze of thin Chinese porcelain. Limehouse glaze was dirty and speckled, and looked messy alongside real Chinese porcelain. After two years of production, the factory was bankrupt and the partners in the Limehouse venture went their separate ways.

A Limehouse sauceboat, 18.8 cm long, c. 1746–8. With cartoon-like painted chinamen, this sophisticated silver shape has become a whimsical novelty.

One of the proprietors from Limehouse took their ideas, designs and know-how to Bristol. The proprietor of the new factory was Benjamin Lund and the Bristol Porcelain Company is known today as Lund's Bristol. As at Limehouse, sauceboats, creamboats and pickle dishes remained the staple productions. The only difference was that the glaze was now

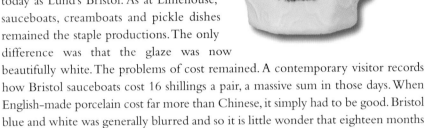

beautifully white. The problems of cost remained. A contemporary visitor records how Bristol sauceboats cost 16 shillings a pair, a massive sum in those days. When English-made porcelain cost far more than Chinese, it simply had to be good. Bristol blue and white was generally blurred and so it is little wonder that eighteen months later Benjamin Lund faced bankruptcy too.

Bow, meanwhile, managed to get things right. Bow made blue and white that looked remarkably like the everyday Chinese porcelain of the time. We have little evidence of how much it sold for, but Bow porcelain must have been competitive or nobody would have bought it. Bow made a great many blue and white plates. The designs looked the part, but the plates themselves were thicker than Chinese porcelain plates. Bow also managed to match the colouring of Chinese porcelain

Two small Bow dishes for sweetmeats or pickle, 12 cm wide, c. 1756–60. The example on the right is painted with one of the best-known Bow patterns, called the 'Golfer and Caddy' for obvious reasons.

A Bow milk jug inscribed in blue under the base, 'W. Pether May 10 1753', 8 cm high. When he painted this jug, Pether was a young apprentice at Bow aged fifteen or sixteen.

glaze. Bow's blue varies enormously in tone, probably because they tried out different sources of cobalt oxide. Around 1749–50 the factory developed a tone of underglaze blue that was a vibrant, almost turquoise blue. A few years later they had reverted back to a darker, inky blue. Collectors learn to distinguish subtle differences in the colour of glaze and blue as they study the chronology of the different factories.

When making blue and white, Bow were price-sensitive and avoided elaborately moulded shapes. Their sauceboats and teapots were generally plain, without embossed cartouches. They copied some complex and intricate Chinese blue and white patterns, but mostly they chose to make a small number of relatively ordinary designs. A Chinaman sitting on a rock with his legs crossed, a heron standing by a banana tree, a dragon flying through clouds. These were copied exactly from Chinese prototypes. Bow's copies are so faithful, they beg the question: did customers in London know they were buying Bow, or did they think they were purchasing real Chinese? The Chinese patterns painted on Bow were just as mysterious as the Orient. One of the best-known patterns shows two Chinese figures standing together in a garden. The taller figure holds a ceremonial sceptre known as a *ruyi* while a smaller figure or boy holds a bundle of rolled-up sacred scrolls. In the eighteenth century at the Bow factory patterns like this were known as 'Image' patterns. In the modern age collectors like to give names to their patterns and this popular Image pattern is called the 'Golfer and Caddy'. Purists know that a *ruyi* sceptre is not a golf club, but a catchy name amuses collectors who know perfectly well this isn't the original eighteenth-century name.

The names of the craftsmen responsible for blue and white painting in England are unknown apart from a single artist at Bow. A simple jug survives painted in blue with the inscription underneath, 'William Pether May 10 1753'. When he painted his jug, Pether was a young apprentice at the Bow china factory. He went on to become a highly talented engraver and was a partner in a printing business with Thomas Frye, the proprietor of the Bow factory. Pether's jug shows that though blue and white was created by junior decorators, the painters who executed these simple patterns could still become highly talented artists in their own right.

While the output of blue and white at Bow was indeed impressive, by comparison the Worcester factory was far more prolific. Curiously, the most important maker of English blue and white almost failed at the very outset. Archaeological excavations have shown that the earliest production at the new Worcester factory was a series of plates and dishes precisely copying Chinese blue and white. The few that survive today are thick and unevenly glazed and are definitely inferior to the Chinese. In order to survive, the partners in the Worcester factory merged with Benjamin Lund's ailing Bristol porcelain factory. This gave Worcester access to Bristol's soaprock recipe. By changing the firing method Worcester overcame Bristol's problem with blurring, and the future of the factory was assured.

Worcester blue and white was durable and soon built a reputation for reliability. It didn't have to pretend to be Chinese and could simply be itself. Limehouse and Bristol had started a tradition for combining Chinese blue and white painting with the shapes of English silver, and Worcester chose to continue with this. The control of the glazing was much advanced and this meant the finely detailed modelling remained clear and sharp on every piece. Between 1752 and 1755 sauceboats were the most important production in blue and white Worcester, along with smaller creamboats. Cream was a luxury in the seventeenth century and was served mixed

A Worcester silver-shaped sauceboat painted with a popular Chinese pattern, 19.3 cm long, workman's mark, c. 1756–7. The factory made a huge number of sauceboats, the shape becoming more stylised and less exciting as time went on.

with expensive powdered sugar. Pouring sweetened cream onto fruit from a Worcester porcelain creamboat or cream jug was a pastime of the well-to-do.

Later in the 1750s tea sets became an incredibly valuable production. There is no denying that Worcester teapots were vastly superior to Chinese porcelain teapots of the time. Worcester teapots were thinner and the spouts were moulded with a graceful curve that, with their coarse straight spouts, the Chinese could not match. Worcester teapots poured beautifully without drips, and the soaprock (or steatitic) formula meant Worcester could guarantee its teapots would not crack when filled with hot water. Their cups and saucers were also the best available in Britain. Coloured Worcester porcelain was still very costly, but blue and white Worcester was now more affordable and could be used every day, giving enormous pleasure to its original owners.

In 1764 the *Oxford Journal* wrote of 'the extraordinary strength and cheapness of the common sort of blue and white Worcester porcelain', adding that it was 'calculated by ease of purchase, for general and ordinary use'. A new invention made sure Worcester blue and white remained competitive. Transfer printing was set to revolutionise the ceramics industry in Britain. The novelty of the process appealed to customers and meant that mugs of Worcester porcelain could be decorated with very detailed patterns of popular garden flowers, landscapes and even portraits of the King and Queen.

A Worcester teapot painted with the 'Gazebo' pattern, 11 cm high, workman's mark, c. 1756. It is beautifully proportioned, thinly potted, evenly glazed, and it pours very well. In the world of porcelain teapots this is close to perfection.

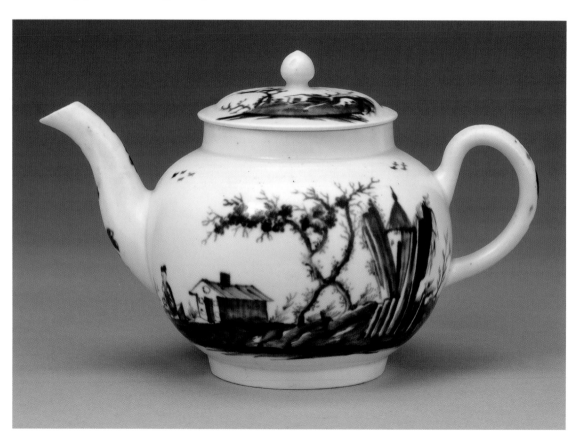

Instead of only importing Chinese blue and white, Britain now enjoyed its own export trade, selling blue and white Worcester to Holland, Germany, France and the Americas. Some Worcester blue and white even found its way to China, for around 1770–5 Chinese porcelain copies were made of popular Worcester salad bowls and fruit drainers, the Chinese making hand-painted copies of Worcester's printed designs.

It wasn't only the Chinese that copied blue and white Worcester. All over Britain other factories made blue and white and most copied Worcester in some way. Espionage was rife. Richard Holdship, who had been closely involved with the development of printing at Worcester, went to Derby where rather unsuccessful blue printing was attempted. There was never a large production of blue and white at Derby but some attractive pierced fruit baskets survive to tell their story. Some blue and white previously believed to have been made at Derby has recently been re-attributed to Isleworth. Joseph Shore learnt the secrets of porcelain manufacture at Worcester in the 1750s. By 1760 he was in partnership with other former Worcester workmen, making their own blue and white porcelain on the banks of the Thames at Isleworth.

Derby and Isleworth both copied Worcester's designs, but although Richard Holdship and Joseph Shore and his colleagues stole some of Worcester's secrets, they didn't have access to soaprock. Robert Podmore was different. He had worked with Dr Wall to develop Worcester porcelain and knew all about Worcester's secret ingredient. Podmore went to Liverpool and sold Worcester's secrets to Richard Chaffers. He also helped Chaffers acquire a licence to mine soaprock in Cornwall. Chaffers' Liverpool porcelain is steatitic and very similar in appearance to Worcester. Chaffers' factory made porcelain in competition with Worcester, but it also faced direct competition from other china factories in Liverpool, all making their own blue and white.

ABOVE LEFT
A Derby dessert basket combining a European shape with a Chinese subject, 22.5 cm wide, c. 1765.

ABOVE
An Isleworth cream jug with underglaze blue printed decoration, 8 cm high, c. 1765–70. The proprietors of the Isleworth factory had learnt the secret of blue printing while working at Worcester.

A Liverpool cup and saucer made by Richard Chaffers & Co., the saucer 11.1 cm in diameter, c. 1758–60. The 'Jumping Boy' was one of Chaffers' most successful patterns.

It is only recently that the different Liverpool porcelains can be identified, thanks to archaeological finds. William Reid and Co. made very similar shapes and patterns to Richard Chaffers, but Reid used a phosphatic (bone ash) formula, which gave a distinctive dark grey-blue colour. Samuel Gilbody's short-lived Liverpool factory is probably the rarest of all English blue and white. Gilbody made copies of Chinese patterns using a very pale tone of underglaze blue. The confused story of Liverpool porcelain gets even more complicated after 1770. Three different members of the same family ran rival china factories in the city. James Pennington continued William Reid's business on Brownlow Hill, while Seth Pennington took over from Philip Christian & Co. who had continued Richard Chaffers' factory on Shaw's Brow. Meanwhile John Pennington made porcelain at Copperas Hill, moving to Folly Lane, all in Liverpool. Little wonder that the blue and white made at each of the three Pennington family factories is hard to tell apart. In keeping with the times, the porcelain made by the Penningtons during the 1770s to '90s is commercial, crude and coarse with only occasional highlights.

It is far easier to recognise other English blue and white factories, as their wares are so very individual. In London, Vauxhall porcelain is distinguished by its wet-looking glaze and distinctive, bright tone of underglaze blue. This has been described

A cream jug from Seth Pennington's factory, 10.5 cm wide, c. 1785–90. The 'biting snake' handle is a distinctive Liverpool feature, although it is not unique to Seth Pennington.

as 'sticky blue' – an appropriate term, for Vauxhall blue and white does look as though it has been freshly painted and has yet to dry out. Vauxhall porcelain was made in a factory where delft had been made previously and this helps explain the appearance of some Vauxhall blue painting, featuring European landscapes with delft-like 'sponged trees'.

A Vauxhall small mug or coffee can painted in a distinctive tone known as 'sticky blue' 7.2 cm high, c. 1755–8. The delft-like, European style painting includes 'sponged trees', a speciality of Vauxhall.

In view of its provincial location in East Anglia, it is hardly surprising that Lowestoft porcelain is one of the most individual English factories. Where else would you find a mug painted with a scene of bathing huts on the local beach? (see the illustration on page 18) Production was never on a large scale but Lowestoft was a curious survivor for it lasted more than forty years, far longer than Chelsea, Bow or Longton Hall. Lowestoft did its share of copying Chinese porcelain and Worcester too, even to the extent of forging Worcester factory marks. The exciting thing about Lowestoft blue and white is the spontaneous nature of the painting. In its first few years especially, from 1759–62, Lowestoft blue and white is painted with a cartoon-like freshness that is quite unique. Comical birds hover in impossible flight while a matchstick Chinaman walks a tightrope between fanciful rococo scrolls. All tremendous fun.

Lowestoft was still making some individual blue and white twenty-five years later: mugs and inkwells inscribed 'A Trifle from Lowestoft' (see page 18) were local seaside souvenirs to sell to visitors. By the 1780s and '90s most of the factory's output was derivative, however. Towards the end of the eighteenth century Lowestoft made much the same shapes and patterns as all of its remaining

Caughley miniature or 'toy' tewares painted with the 'Island' pattern, c. 1785–90. The coffee pot is 8.5 cm high. Caughley made an extensive range of miniature porcelain 'toys' as playthings for adults as well as children.

competitors in Britain, struggling to compete with very much cheaper imported Chinese porcelain. Factories like Bow and Vauxhall had closed down many years before. Derby had given up blue and white and Worcester was on the point of giving up underglaze blue as a decoration on its own. After 1785 taste had changed and customers didn't want simple painted blue and white patterns. Transfer printing meant very complicated designs were available. Pottery, in the form of thin 'pearlware' plates from Staffordshire, was new competition, and some of this Staffordshire pottery was printed with busy patterns such as the 'Willow Pattern'. Most English porcelain factories could not begin to match these for price.

Of the makers of traditional 'soft paste' porcelain, only Caughley put up a fight and still made inexpensive blue and white. The Caughley porcelain factory was established by Thomas Turner who had worked at Worcester as a senior manager and understood precisely what kind of porcelain customers wanted to buy. Turner left Worcester around 1772 to set up a rival factory further up the river Severn at Caughley near Bridgnorth. Turner took many Worcester workmen with him and they knew the secret of making soaprock porcelain. Caughley made identical shapes and patterns to Worcester, but instead of costly coloured and gilded porcelain, Caughley specialised almost entirely in blue and white. As well as copying Worcester's most popular patterns, Caughley used transfer printing to make the intense and complex Chinese landscape patterns the public wanted to buy in the 1780s and '90s. They also made pretty little shapes that were not available from China, such as pickle dishes, wine tasters, asparagus servers and eyebaths. These are particularly popular with collectors today, along with an extensive range of miniature porcelain for children to play with.

After fifty exciting years, English blue and white porcelain had reached the end of its natural life. Times had moved on and Worcester's once secret process of printing in underglaze blue was now available to everyone. The Staffordshire pottery industry, led by Josiah Spode, used printing on earthenware to supply dining rooms and tea tables all over the world. Some Staffordshire porcelain makers, such as Miles Mason, made printed porcelain versions of Chinese blue and white tea sets. Blue and white was now a mass-production, factory process and after 1800 products lack the charm that makes early English blue and white so appealing and collectable.

Chapter Three

THE LONDON TASTE: 1750–70

IN THE middle of the eighteenth century, a visit to the Ranelagh Gardens in Chelsea was a chance for London's society ladies to show off their latest fashions as they walked among the trees, tea stalls and traders hawking their wares. Likewise a visit to fashionable St James's for window-shopping in the jewellers and emporiums gave a chance to browse the exotic goods imported from all corners of the globe. Silks, spices and porcelain from the Orient were readily available at a price. Even more costly, though, was a very different kind of porcelain. William and Mary Deards owned a shop at the end of Pall Mall near St James's and the Haymarket. In 1751 they advertised for sale:

> all sorts of Jewels, Watches, Plate, and all other curious Work in Gold, Silver, and Gilt, Dresden & all other Fine China, Variety of fine Toys, and all Curiosities in General.

The Deards sold Japanese and Chinese porcelain, but their most valuable chinaware was imported from Dresden. Meanwhile the 'fine Toys' listed in their advertisement will have included porcelain novelties made in London, at Chelsea and nearby in St James's.

Chinese porcelain was bought for general use. Porcelain from Dresden was far more special. It wasn't available in any great quantity; indeed, trade restrictions prevented direct importations from Germany. Traders in London bought their Dresden from Paris, Rome or even St Petersburg. They approached families in Prussia and Poland to buy their tableware, for old Dresden sold for a high premium. It was amongst the best porcelain money could buy. Its popularity with customers in London was due to fashion. People wanted Dresden simply because it was refreshingly different. Dresden didn't look Chinese.

In those days the term Dresden meant porcelain made at the Meissen factory. Meissen was twelve miles from Dresden and in the eighteenth century everyone knew Meissen as the porcelain that came from Dresden. Later, in the nineteenth century, the Dresden name was used much more widely to refer to any porcelain made in the same style. To distinguish their higher-quality products, the Saxon State factory at Meissen reverted to using only the Meissen name.

All of the recently established English porcelain factories realised that the public held Dresden in high esteem and would willingly buy imitations. The problem in England was obtaining specimens to copy of the valuable, real porcelain from Meissen. Fortunately, Nicholas Sprimont had a plan. By 1750 his Chelsea porcelain factory was thriving. At the end of Chelsea's experimental phase (the Triangle period

OPPOSITE
A pair of Derby figures known as 'Ranelagh Dancers', 26 cm high, c. 1765. These depict the kind of fine gentleman and lady you would expect to meet when walking in London's Ranelagh Gardens.

33

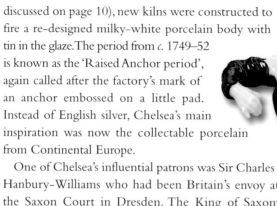

A Chelsea figure of Pantaloon from the commedia dell'arte, *11 cm high, Raised Anchor mark, c. 1750–2. This is a direct copy of a Meissen original, probably one that was borrowed from Sir Charles Hanbury-Williams.*

discussed on page 10), new kilns were constructed to fire a re-designed milky-white porcelain body with tin in the glaze. The period from *c.* 1749–52 is known as the 'Raised Anchor period', again called after the factory's mark of an anchor embossed on a little pad. Instead of English silver, Chelsea's main inspiration was now the collectable porcelain from Continental Europe.

One of Chelsea's influential patrons was Sir Charles Hanbury-Williams who had been Britain's envoy at the Saxon Court in Dresden. The King of Saxony, Augustus III, used porcelain as diplomatic gifts and had presented Hanbury-Williams with a collection of fine Meissen porcelain. Sprimont heard that Sir Charles owned the best collection of Dresden, kept in his home at Holland House in London. By pulling a few strings, influential friends persuaded Sir Charles to lend his entire Dresden collection to the Chelsea factory. By the end of 1751 an extensive range of Chelsea copies was on sale in London and in fashionable society this was the hit of the season.

Rival English porcelain factories at Bow, Derby and Longton Hall jumped on the Dresden bandwagon. Rather than copy Dresden originals, now they could all

BELOW
Two different versions of 'Harlequin and Columbine Dancing', 19.5 cm high, made at Bow (left) and Chelsea (right), c. 1755–8. Both were copied from a Meissen original, but they lost a lot of detail in translation.

copy Chelsea instead. Soon all the factories were making versions of Harlequin and Columbine, copied from each other. The English factories also created some new and original figures of their own. The individuality was down to the skills – or lack of skills – on the part of their modellers.

The Bow factory mostly copied oriental porcelain, but in the early 1750s Dresden-style figures became an important part of their production. They employed a very distinctive modeller whose name is unknown but he has become known as the 'Muses Modeller' after his best-known series of figures of Apollo and the Muses. The Bow factory had only limited access to Meissen prototypes, and so compared with Chelsea's perfect copies of Dresden, the work of the Muses Modeller is decidedly amateur. It does have its own very unique charm as a result. The first porcelain figures made at Longton Hall in Staffordshire also have their own amateur charm, which is partly due to firing problems (the very thick covering of glaze having given their white figures the nickname 'snowmen'). Like those of the Muses Modeller, Longton Hall figures have a naivety that appeals to collectors today.

Early figures made at the Derby factory were superior in so many respects. During what is known as the Planché period (see page 14), Derby figures and groups were special because most were totally original and not copied directly from Meissen. The fine detail and sculptural qualities are best seen when the figures are left in the white. Derby figures from the early 1750s are known as 'Dry Edge' because to

ABOVE LEFT
A Bow figure of Polyhymnia from a set of figures representing the classical Muses, 17 cm high, c. 1750–4. The unknown but distinctive Bow factory sculptor responsible is known as the 'Muses Modeller'.

ABOVE
A Derby figure of a dancer from the 'Dry Edge' period, 17 cm high, c. 1755. This class of figure is so called because during this period, to prevent kiln adhesion, the glaze was wiped away from the edge of the base before firing.

A Chelsea tureen in the shape of a bunch of asparagus, 17.5 cm long, from the Red Anchor period, c. 1755–6. The most important part of a meal was the dessert when trompe l'oeil *tureens featured as table decorations.*

prevent sticking in the kiln the glaze was wiped away from the outer edge of the bases leaving a slightly rough, unglazed margin.

Back at Chelsea, the period from *c.* 1752–8 is known as the 'Red Anchor period' as the mark of a tiny anchor neatly painted in red appears under the footrims of the porcelain or tucked away at the back of the bases of the increasingly elaborate figures that were copied from Meissen or derived from contemporary engravings. Not only figures were copied from Meissen. Tea sets and dinnerware were made in new shapes painted with flowers or birds. The flowers were not the formal peonies or lotus seen on Chinese porcelain of the time. Instead these were recognisable garden flowers familiar to customers in Europe. Meissen had developed the painting style known as *deutsche Blumen* as it depicted German rather than oriental flowers. Artists at Chelsea copied Meissen flower painting directly but they also went much further and developed a unique form of decoration, one of the most splendid of all time.

The most important part of a meal was the dessert, for this was the chance for wealthy homes to show off to their friends. Fresh fruit, cream and sugar were all costly and called for very special porcelain and table decorations. To impress, and also to amuse, curious covered tureens in the forms of animals, birds, fruit or vegetables were placed down the centre of the dining table during the dessert course. This was a Continental tradition that was adopted in Britain and one that Chelsea was particularly keen to supply. *Trompe l'œil* tureens were made by most of the early English china factories. They also made dishes in the shape of flowers and leaves, some constructed most ingeniously.

To accompany the naturalistic splendour of novelty tureens and dishes, plates in Meissen's *deutsche Blumen* pattern were not sufficiently impressive. Instead, Chelsea porcelain took new inspiration from the scientific study in the nearby Chelsea Physic Garden. Painters at the Chelsea factory may have borrowed actual botanical specimens grown in the gardens. Mostly, though, they copied recently published engravings of plants, particularly a series by Philip Miller. We know from contemporary sale catalogues that the Chelsea factory described its new botanical porcelain as painted with Sir Hans Sloane's plants. Sloane was a man of science with a noted interest in botany. He had in fact died a few years before the porcelain was made and Chelsea chose to honour his memory. Sir Hans Sloane decoration is exciting, extremely decorative and, above all, uniquely British.

The Meissen style of porcelain decoration was perfectly suited to the mood of the age, for this was the time of rococo. Named after the French word *rocaille* meaning a shell or grotto, rococo was more than just a style of decorative ornament. The spirit of rococo was reflected in music, theatre and fashion. It was frivolous and fun. In art, rococo was not restricted by symmetry. Curves and scrolling ornament did not have to balance in any conventional sense.

The London china factories of Bow and Chelsea, St James's and a newcomer at Vauxhall all understood rococo and among them made a great deal of delicate porcelain. Modelled rococo scrollwork mirrored English silver shapes and imported European porcelain. A curious sideline to the rococo spirit was the style of ornament known as *chinoiserie*. More Chinese than the real thing, *chinoiserie* was a European fashion using motifs inspired by China and Japan mixed in a whimsical way due to a failure to understand Chinese art and especially perspective in Chinese painting.

Situated a hundred miles from London, Worcester's interpretation of *chinoiserie* had been different to the London factories. In the earlier 1750s there was a ready market for Worcester's Chinese decoration and its blue and white. Once Chelsea had made the Meissen style fashionable, however, Worcester found itself behind the times. Around 1756–7 Worcester changed much of its enamelled decoration to reflect the Meissen fashion. To make their own Meissen-style porcelain Worcester didn't need to borrow and copy a collection of the real thing. Instead Worcester imitated Chelsea porcelain from the Red Anchor period. Worcester's versions were

Two Chelsea botanical plates, 21.8 cm in diameter, c. 1755–6. These took their name and inspiration from Sir Hans Sloane's scientific work in London.

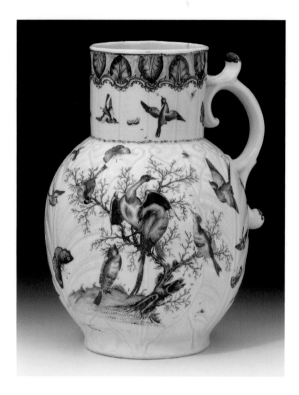

very different to Chelsea's. Chelsea's copies had been as perfect and precise as they could be. Worcester painted the designs more quickly and with more of a cartoon-like spontaneity.

The two other principal factories outside London also copied Chelsea in the Meissen style. Like Worcester, they did it in their own way. The painters at each factory developed their own motifs and mannerisms, which enable collectors to distinguish one from another. Early collectors gave their own names to distinctive styles of painting. Derby collectors, for example, noticed that many Meissen-style flowers, birds and fruit on Derby from the 1755–60 period were accompanied by crazy, fanciful insects. A different style of flower painting on Derby included bouquets where the stems of the flowers were represented by very thin lines no wider than a thread. These two groups were attributed to a 'Moth Painter' and a 'Cotton Stem Painter'. It is clear that these were not single individuals and many painters worked in the Cotton Stem style. The names have stuck, however, and are useful as a means of remembering each factory's different painting styles. Everyone remembers the name of the 'Trembly Rose Painter', even though several different hands painted the distinctive 'trembly' style of flower painting at Longton Hall in Staffordshire.

ABOVE
A Worcester moulded jug known as a 'Dutch Jug' painted with the 'Mobbing Birds' pattern, 26.5 cm high, c. 1760. Loosely derived from Chelsea, the painting instead has a cartoon-like naivety.

RIGHT
A Longton Hall 'Strawberry' pattern moulded dish, 27.5 cm wide, c. 1755–60. The distinctive style of flower painting is named after a 'Trembly Rose Painter' invented by early collectors.

A Chelsea dish painted in the French style, 26 cm wide, c. 1752–4. At this date porcelain from Vincennes had only recently arrived in London in very small quantities. Chelsea saw a chance to capture a new valuable market.

A Chelsea octagonal teabowl and saucer painted with fables, Raised Anchor period, c. 1749–52. Fable subjects and other animal decoration were the speciality of Jefferyes Hammett O'Neale.

By the time Worcester and the others were making Meissen style porcelain, Chelsea had moved on. Alongside their copies of Meissen, Chelsea also copied porcelain from Vincennes, the new royal factory from France and the forerunner of Sèvres. Like Meissen, Vincennes was available in London after 1750 but only in very small quantities. Chelsea clearly borrowed some Vincennes and copied the new style of landscape and flower painting. The colouring was better suited to the soft paste porcelain made in France and looked good on the creamy porcelain produced at Chelsea during the Raised Anchor period.

Some of the artists responsible for copying the European style decoration at Chelsea came from the Continent, including the Duvivier family, but a lack of signed pieces makes it difficult to ascribe actual pieces. One very distinctive decoration is associated with a talented Irish artist. Jefferyes Hammett O'Neale painted animals and was responsible for much of the 'Fable' decoration at Chelsea, popular early in the 1750s. Octagonal-shaped teawares and silver-shaped dishes painted with fables are amongst the most distinctive, and desirable, specimens of early English porcelain.

Louis XV moved his royal French porcelain factory from Vincennes to Sèvres in 1752. Sèvres specialised in the most sumptuous coloured grounds combined with

A Chelsea candlestick figure 27.5 cm high, from the Gold Anchor period, c. 1760. Popular taste called for porcelain with as much rococo scrollwork and floral ornament as possible.

A pair of Bow figures of Harlequin and Columbine, 18 cm high, c. 1765–70. Later Bow figures follow the fashion for elaborate bocage *and are frequently raised on rococo scroll feet.*

luscious fruit and flower painting as well as painted birds and figure subjects. This new style of decoration had enormous influence on the rest of Europe. At Chelsea, Sèvres replaced Meissen as the principal design influence. This was during the 'Gold Anchor period', the final phase of the Chelsea factory from 1758 into the 1760s. Chelsea really took rococo to heart and instead of simply copying Sèvres shapes, London modellers created their own eccentric vase shapes. Within reserved panels, artists including John Donaldson painted figure subjects as fine as any French specimens. Coloured grounds proved difficult to control during the firing but Chelsea made up for these with tooled gilding of the highest quality.

Figure making at Chelsea also moved with the times. The factory's principal modeller, Joseph Williams, adapted some of the latest Meissen figures and also created many totally original subjects. During the Gold Anchor period Chelsea added as much rococo scrollwork as they could possibly fit onto each figure group, together with extraordinary porcelain trees awash with modelled flowers and blossom. Flowering trees and branches, known as *bocage*, became a crucial part of all English porcelain figures as fashion called for more and more elaborate ornaments in British homes.

Chelsea porcelain had an enormous influence on all other English china factories. Derby and Bow became significant makers of figures. Both copied many Chelsea or Meissen prototypes, while other models were original and unique to each. Fashion meant that all figures became more elaborate. The plain, mound bases popular in the 1750s gained fancy scrollwork around the edges. By the mid 1760s and into the 1770s fancy bases became the norm. Later Bow figures were frequently raised on four rococo scroll feet, while Derby added trees behind their popular models.

Because Worcester excelled at making durable tea sets, plates and dishes, they did not feel the need to make more than a handful of figures. The influence of Sèvres encouraged Worcester to try out new coloured grounds but they shared Chelsea's problems with firing even backgrounds, yellow and green proving particularly tricky. Chelsea had great trouble with their solid underglaze blue ground, known as 'Mazarine', as it dribbled and ran with the glassy glaze. Bow had developed 'powder blue', blowing a fine powder of cobalt oxide onto their porcelain before glazing to produce an even, slightly granular background. Worcester used powder blue also but still had problems with blurring. They overcame the problem at Worcester by inventing 'scale blue'. This involved a painter drawing a fine scale pattern in underglaze blue onto the porcelain background. Although time consuming, the result was a well-controlled blue background with an interesting scale texture that proved popular.

Worcester's scale blue was a huge success and the vast output was nothing short of mass production. Panels of colourful painted flowers, or so-called 'Fancy Birds' were framed with gold scrollwork patterns in the rococo taste. The reserved panels

A Worcester bell-shaped mug with a 'scale blue' ground, 12 cm high, square mark, c. 1768–72. The panels of 'Fancy Birds' are framed with rococo scrollwork in tooled gold.

A Worcester mug printed with a portrait of Frederick, King of Prussia, 8.4 cm high, signed 'RH Worcester' for the engraver Robert Hancock, dated 1757 and with a printed anchor rebus for the Holdship Brothers. Printing on porcelain was Worcester's greatest invention.

on Worcester's scale blue followed the cartouche shapes of fancy mirrors that decorated the most fashionable rococo rooms in grand houses. On a technical level Worcester's scale blue plates and tea sets were superb productions, but artistically they lost much of the frivolity that rococo needs in order to be exciting.

Worcester's method of mass production meant making vast quantities of a smaller number of set-patterns, whether in blue and white or in rich colours and gilding. Transfer printing was their greatest invention and this produced perfect decoration every time. The factory in Worcester sold their porcelain through a London warehouse and it was widely exported, especially to the Netherlands and to America. It sold well, but somehow Worcester porcelain from 1770 lacks all the spontaneity that collectors love about the factory's productions from fifteen years earlier. Other porcelain factories in England followed the same directions as Worcester and copied their patterns. What had become a thriving British industry was in danger of stagnating, at a time when severe economic recession was about to grip the country.

Thank goodness a small, independent china painter in London was on hand to save the day. Even though he did not manufacture chinaware himself, James Giles made a bigger contribution to the English porcelain industry in eighteenth-century Britain than almost anyone else. The great thing about James Giles is that he was based in London in the middle of the most fashionable retail area. What is more, he sold his decorated porcelain directly to the public. He observed at first hand what sort of china the well-to-do ladies in London wanted to buy, and he gave them what they wanted.

Chapter Four

A TIME OF CHANGE: 1770–90

IT HARDLY seems credible that the great Chelsea factory could fail. Proprietor Nicholas Sprimont blamed ill health and gave up in 1770. His rival, William Duesbury of Derby, acquired what remained of the Chelsea business. Just a few years earlier the Vauxhall factory had become bankrupt and the owner Nicholas Crisp faced further ruin after an ill-fated attempt to move his business to Bovey Tracy in Devon. Longton Hall had closed back in 1760 and William Littler, the proprietor, had moved to Scotland. The porcelain he made at West Pans near Musselbrough was an inferior version of his earlier work at Longton Hall and this also proved unsuccessful. The kilns at West Pans were shut early in the 1770s. Even the Worcester factory was in trouble and in 1772 the manufactory was put up for sale. Worse was to come, for by 1775 porcelain production had ended at Bow. In less than a decade so much changed in the story of English porcelain.

Wars in Europe and in America fuelled a severe economic recession in Britain and the luxury-goods industry was badly affected. Instead of buying costly English porcelain, customers chose cheaper Chinese imports. There was also a new alternative in the form of fine pottery. In 1770 Josiah Wedgwood and Thomas Bentley opened their new pottery factory at Etruria in Staffordshire. Wedgwood was an astute businessman and with the help of patronage from the Queen, his London showroom persuaded society ladies to choose Queensware, his name for thin, cream-coloured earthenware. Wedgwood also led a revolutionary change in public taste.

Chelsea's customers had lived for rococo. Even when they wanted figures with a classical theme, their gods and heroes were usually accompanied by fancy scrollwork and dainty modelled flowers. All of this suddenly changed. The Adams Brothers, the influential Scottish architects, led public taste in a grand, new direction. They worshipped the buildings of ancient Rome, epitomised by the Pantheon with its columns and symmetrical dome. Romanesque ornament was also dominated by symmetry. Students of art, energetic young gentlemen and even society ladies all went on the 'Grand Tour' to see the ancient sites of Greece and Italy. They toured the excavations at Pompeii and Herculaneum and they came back with their own souvenirs in the form of ancient urns and statuary. They then asked the Adams Brothers to re-model their stately British houses in the neo-classical taste.

Fashion changed quickly in London and china makers struggled to keep up. Once again it was Chelsea that led the way, but now under new management. Nicholas Sprimont, as noted above, retired on health grounds, but as he had been one of the greatest exponents of rococo design, his heart probably wasn't in the new taste. William Duesbury who bought the Chelsea works continued to use the London

OPPOSITE
A Derby figure of a shepherd, 34 cm high, with incised factory mark and N396, c. 1785–90. Biscuit figures require superior modelling and Derby engaged leading sculptors from the Continent to create new subjects.

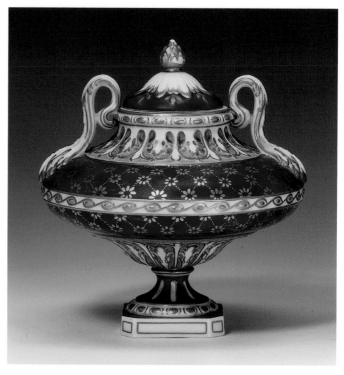

ABOVE
A West Pans mug with a distinctive 'Littler's Blue' ground, 15.2 cm high, c. 1765–70. The blurred decoration and lack of fired gilding are West Pans characteristics.

ABOVE
A Chelsea-Derby vase in the neo-classical taste, 18 cm high, with gold anchor marks, c. 1770. While the shape derives from ancient Rome, the colouring follows the latest London fashion.

A Worcester plate decorated in the Giles workshop, 19.2 cm in diameter, c. 1770. James Giles copied his painting styles from the latest Meissen porcelain.

premises and now ran them in conjunction with his Derby china factory. Because it is difficult to determine which products were made at which factory, the period from 1770 to 1784 is known as 'Chelsea-Derby'. Duesbury understood the London marketplace and made the brave switch to neo-classical porcelain. He possibly took his lead from the independent London decorator James Giles, who in turn followed closely the latest imported European porcelain from Meissen, Sèvres and Naples. Duesbury's factories made new shapes that were seen as highly original designs, while Giles painted on Worcester porcelain 'blanks'. We like to think Giles's spontaneous and freely drawn flower painting was his own invention, but all it takes is a cursory examination of Meissen from the 'Academic' or 'Dot' period (1764–73) to realise that Giles was doing nothing new. He simply copied the latest Meissen styles and sold it to customers who saw it as refreshingly different. Because of wars in Europe and trade restrictions, customers still had problems buying imported china from the Continent, so they were happy to buy copies painted in London.

The Chelsea-Derby factories and James Giles's workshop were both responsible for some very smart and tasteful neo-classical decoration. Elegant wheels and medallions called *paterae* were linked by swags of formal foliage to rams' heads and cows' skulls (*bucrania*). In the middle of plates and dishes the china painters copied images of ancient marble urns, a different classical vase on each piece. Portrait medallions in cameo simulated ancient gems carved with the profile heads of the Roman emperors. All this should have proved popular in London, but times were now desperate for the British economy.

A pair of Chelsea-Derby plates, 22.2 cm in diameter, with gold anchor marks, c. 1775–80. The stunning design incorporates popular neo-classical motifs of ancient urns and portrait medallions.

The great Worcester factory had enjoyed many years of success, but the recession hit them hard. They still made wonderful porcelain, but they suffered perhaps from being so far from London and were set in their ways. Their 'scale blue' porcelain was totally rococo but not as lively as Chelsea. When public taste changed to classical, Worcester's richest porcelain stopped selling. Worcester continued to copy Chinese and Japanese designs, offering to match any porcelain patterns from the Orient that customers needed, and their teapots still proved popular because they didn't break (see page 26). The problem now, in the 1770s, was that the price of Chinese imported porcelain had fallen. Worcester's blue and white was still the mainstay of the factory's production but once Chinese blue and white was cheaper, demand for Worcester copies fell. Dr Wall and many of the original partners in the Worcester business were of an advanced age. In 1772 Wall retired and the factory was sold to a new partnership, still headed by his friend William Davis who was also getting on in years.

For the next fifteen years Worcester remained stubbornly set in their ways. They stuck with rococo for far too long and when Worcester did eventually copy some neo-classical designs from Giles and Chelsea-Derby they were in production ten years too late. One area where Worcester did enjoy success was in enamelled porcelain in the French taste. Curiously, it is unlikely that Worcester actually copied their new patterns directly from Sèvres, for Chelsea-Derby made similar shapes and designs at the same time and rather better in terms of quality of workmanship. Worcester, however, made a range of colourful, symmetrical patterns typified by the 'Hop Trellis' designs. Garlands of berried foliage entwined around formal garden trellises had been painted on Sèvres porcelain since the 1760s. A distinctive shape of teacup and teapot with vertical ribbing was also made in France twenty years before Worcester introduced their 'French' shape, but it was in the 1780s that the robust nature of Worcester's Sèvres-style enamelling enjoyed popularity in Britain.

The business arrangement between the Worcester factory and James Giles to supply white porcelain became strained and by the 1770s the two concerns had become rivals. With an unreliable supply of white porcelain and relying only on the luxury end of the London market, Giles was bankrupt in 1775. The Bow factory closed at around the same time, a victim of cheaper Chinese imported porcelain and an inability to adapt to classical designs.

This may not seem to have been a good time for a new venture into the experimental area of English 'true' porcelain but following several years of trial and error at Plymouth, William Cookworthy and Richard Champion were responsible for a new factory at Castle

A Worcester spoon tray, 16.8 cm wide, c. 1775–80. The popularity of French fashion encouraged Worcester to copy a wide range of Sèvres patterns including the 'Hop Trellis' design.

A Champion's Bristol cup and saucer, which bear painted crossed swords and dot marks in underglaze blue on their undersides, c. 1775. Bristol's hard paste porcelain looked like Meissen and they purposely copied Meissen patterns, along with the Meissen crossed-swords factory mark.

Green in Bristol. Commencing in 1770, Champion's Bristol factory used kaolin (china clay) and feldspar to make so-called hard paste porcelain. Chemically this was similar to Chinese porcelain and it was also similar to Meissen and other German porcelain. Imported Chinese porcelain was now readily available in Britain and there was no financial advantage in copying the wares of the Orient. Instead Bristol porcelain looked to imitate the famous Meissen china. Richard Champion invested heavily in obtaining patents to exploit the commercial potential of Cookworthy's invention. At Bristol, Champion copied directly some of the shapes and patterns from Meissen. Bristol porcelain was marked with a cross to look like Meissen, and some Bristol is even marked with exact copies of the crossed swords and dot marks used at Meissen during the Academic Period. Sadly, though, Bristol porcelain could not be made economically and while Champion was entrenched in legal battles with Josiah Wedgwood to protect his patent, his china business failed. The works at Bristol closed in 1781.

Porcelain manufacture continued at Lowestoft and at several small factories in Liverpool but in these cases it was never on a large scale. Lowestoft survived by imitating the established wares of Worcester and copying Chinese porcelain and selling these to a local market rather than attempting to compete in London. By contrast Liverpool porcelain was mostly exported. During the 1770s the Pennington family increased production of blue and white tea sets, sacrificing quality control in favour of cheap prices in an attempt to compete with inexpensive Chinese porcelain. Lowestoft and Liverpool porcelains were old-fashioned but found a ready market because they were inexpensive.

Derby survived because it was now the only English factory making figures and also because it had adapted to the new classical taste. Worcester failed on both counts and only survived the 1770s on the strength of its blue and white. Worcester had perfected transfer printing on porcelain, and their underglaze blue-printed tea and

A Lowestoft teapot painted with the 'Dolls House' pattern, 14 cm high, c. 1780–5. This copies a Chinese version of an older Japanese Imari pattern. At Lowestoft this colouring is known as 'Redgrave' decoration after a local family who painted at the factory.

dinner sets sold well, particularly in Holland. Worcester's sales manager and former engraver, Thomas Turner, defected (see page 31), and in 1775 was producing blue and white in competition, further up the River Severn at Caughley. While at Worcester, Turner had learnt that expensive ornamental porcelain was not profitable and realised that during a time of economic hardship middle-class customers wanted to use less costly porcelain services. Thomas Turner's Caughley factory concentrated on mass-produced underglaze blue-printing, in direct competition with his former employers at Worcester.

A teapot from Seth Pennington's Liverpool factory, inscribed and dated 1783. Most Liverpool porcelain was exported but this piece was made for a local customer. Mary Sharples lived in the nearby town of Lodge.

Towards the end of the eighteenth century competition in England came to a head. Factories only survived by specialising in the area of the marketplace that they best understood. Worcester and Derby decided to go up-market, abandoning cheap blue and white and inexpensive teawares in favour of the highest quality in terms of decoration and design. Up-to-date fashion from France provided Derby and Worcester with new tasteful designs, always finished off most carefully with the best gilding. Thankfully, wealthy customers were more than happy to pay for the best quality.

Derby closed its London manufactory and some of the best London decorators moved to Derby. Instead of relying just on its established workforce, Derby employed new talented artists both as painters and as sculptors. Figure modellers from France and from the Tournai factory in Belgium included J.J. Spengler and Pierre Stephan. Alongside old-fashioned rococo shepherds and shepherdesses, Derby now made classical figure subjects and new allegorical groups seen at their best when issued as plain white, unglazed sculptures. Derby Biscuit or 'bisque' was exciting but costly. It appealed to the upper classes, who became Derby's principal customers.

Derby still made a phosphatic porcelain (containing bone ash), which was unreliable when used for making tea or serving hot food. Derby tea sets and dessert services were generally for decoration only and just to show off. Elegant border patterns in the French style were neatly edged with fine gilding. Customers wanted dark blue borders, which were difficult to make in England. Derby developed a very rich blue enamel used overglaze, which became known as 'Smith's Blue' and is very distinctive. In the centres of cups, saucers and plates, delightful landscape scenes were painted by Zachariah Boreman, while Richard Askew painted little Cupids flying in clouds and Edward Withers painted delicate flowers and fruit sprigs.

A Caughley printed mug, 11.9 cm high, dated under the base 25 July 1794. Caughley mass-produced blue-printed porcelain in competition with Worcester. This mug depicts a local landmark, the Ironbrige a few miles from the Caughley factory.

A Chelsea-Derby teapot painted with Cupids by Richard Askew, 11 cm high, with gold anchor and D mark, c. 1775. Copied from Meissen, this was the ultimate taste in fine porcelain in London and would have formed part of a costly cabaret.

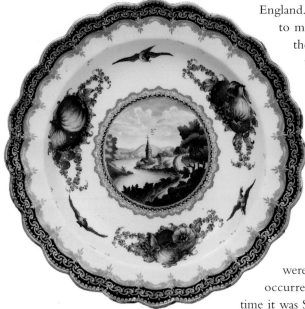

A Worcester plate of 'Lord Henry Thynne' pattern, 21.5 cm in diameter, c. 1780–5. Boldly painted in thick enamel colours, a full dessert service would have been made to impress.

Derby was now the market leader in fine porcelain in England. At Worcester William Davis and Co. continued to make cheap blue and white printed patterns into the 1780s while their more costly coloured wares were, for the most part, disappointing copies of Derby. Worcester's famous scale blue was replaced with patterns featuring underglaze blue borders that copied the look of the Smith's Blue borders at Derby. Davis and his partners lost heart and sold the business to the manager of their London warehouse. Thomas Flight bought the Worcester factory in 1783 but ignored its problems until his sons were old enough to take control. Meanwhile the factory desperately needed new direction.

While the makers of fine porcelain in England were struggling to find their feet, significant changes occurred at the opposite end of the marketplace. This time it was Staffordshire's turn to lead the way in producing cheaper porcelain for general use. By the 1780s the many pottery manufacturers in the towns around Stoke-on-Trent had perfected creamware and were working on new kinds of refined earthenwares and stoneware. Their main competition was also the cheaper Chinese porcelain that was now imported into Europe in ever increasing quantities. In a brave attempt to challenge this competition, the New Hall China factory was established in 1781 by a partnership of Staffordshire pottery manufacturers. These potters hoped to use Richard Champion's hard paste formula from his failed venture at Bristol, but the porcelain they eventually made at New Hall was very different to the 'true' porcelain of Germany and France. In basic terms the New Hall porcelain mixed the hard paste formula of kaolin and feldspar with other kinds of clay and bone ash. This is generally referred to today as a 'hybrid hard paste' porcelain.

The aim of the New Hall factory was to compete with cheap Chinese imports by mass-producing tea and coffee sets. New Hall made a surprisingly small number of different shapes and a very organised range of set patterns. Designs mostly copied the *famille rose* border patterns that flooded into Europe from China. They also imitated simple French patterns copied from Paris porcelain, as well as occasional richer Japan or Imari styles. New Hall didn't make vases or figures and avoided designs that were purely ornamental. Instead their porcelain was functional above all else and their tea sets were intended for everyday use. To help china dealers place repeat orders, the New Hall factory pioneered the use of pattern numbers, neatly painted in red underneath the bases of its tea sets. These pattern numbers are a huge help to collectors today, assisting with identification of New Hall shapes.

New Hall was very successful and had its imitators. Many other small china factories were established in Staffordshire and elsewhere, making copies of New Hall shapes and producing very similar patterns. They did not use factory marks

A Staffordshire teapot with a copy of a Chinese export pattern, 14.5 cm high, c. 1790. This was made by one of many unidentified factories contemporary with New Hall.

and although there are clues in the sequences of pattern numbers they each used, not all of these other makers can be identified. Pioneering work was carried out in the 1970s by David Holgate, Geoffrey Godden and others to sort out which factory made each different shape of teapots, cups and jugs. To assist collectors, distinctive groups of porcelains in the New Hall style were designated the names Factory X, Factory Y and Factory Z. Thirty years on it is clear that there were many more than three contemporary factories involved. Some have now been identified – Factory X is almost certainly Keeling & Co. – but the X, Y and Z names are still widely used.

As the eighteenth century came to an end, English porcelain manufacturers were divided into two very different camps. At one extreme were Worcester and Derby, making the best luxury porcelain aimed at wealthy customers. In complete contrast, New Hall and other Staffordshire porcelain makers supplied the china shops of Britain with a basic and affordable product. These two different directions were set to continue as the nineteenth century dawned.

Two New Hall teapots with contrasting patterns, the shape known at the time as 'Comode', 24 cm long, marked with pattern numbers 167 and 421, c. 1795–1805. New Hall offered customers a wide choice of set patterns to suit every taste.

Chapter Five

REGENCY SPLENDOUR: 1790–1840

Painting on porcelain is unlike any other kind of art. You do not apply paints in their proper colours as you go along, blending and mixing different tones and textures. Ceramic colours involve complex chemical reactions as the fire of the kiln melts the glassy porcelain glaze. To manufacture ceramic colours, different metal oxides are combined with coloured glass as a flux and then crushed into fine powder. Mixed with oil these can look like ordinary oil paints, but they behave totally differently when painted onto the glass-like surface of porcelain. In the intense heat of the kiln most colours change completely. The glaze softens and the powdered glass and metal oxides melt and flow together, sealing the colours on top of the glaze as the fired porcelain cools. The result is permanent and smooth, but there are added complications. Not only do the colours change in the firing, not all colours mature or fuse at the same temperature.

It takes many years of patient training to learn how to paint on porcelain. Ceramic artists are taught to predict the way colours will react, and how to build up layers of different pigments over a succession of different kiln firings. A finely detailed painted panel on a vase or plate can take many days or even weeks of work spread over as many as ten separate kiln firings. Gilding is then the final stage of the decorating process. Bright gold can be applied in a single firing, but if you want raised ornament or texture to your gold, this can also involve a series of different kiln firings, building up layers of paste and applying thick gold on top. After all of this, fired gilding emerges from the kiln looking dull and lifeless. To make it shine the surface of the goldwork has to be 'burnished' or polished to give it the right brilliance and texture.

To appreciate a piece of fine antique porcelain, it is important to understand how it was made and to comprehend just how much skilled and time-consuming work has gone into the decoration. The finely painted and gilded porcelain made at Worcester and Derby in the years either side of 1800 was enormously expensive. It can be costly when bought by collectors today, but in real terms and considering the buying-power of money then and now, this finest English porcelain cost its owners far more when it was new than it costs us to buy it today. During the 1780s the Derby factory realised that the nobility and gentry had riches to spare and that customers would pay princely sums for very special pieces of porcelain. Chelsea had learnt this and engaged experienced artists to paint the reserved panels on its best vases. After the closure of the old Chelsea works in 1784 at the end of the Chelsea-Derby Period, William Duesbury brought some of the most talented artists to Derby where they trained and inspired other painters.

OPPOSITE
A very large Derby vase of a shape known as a 'Long Tom', the splendid flower painting so typical of Regency taste, 62 cm high, red painted factory mark, c. 1825

*A Derby cabinet cup
and saucer, the front
panel painted with 'Una',
factory marks painted
in blue, c. 1790–5.
The Derby factory pattern
book records that James
Banford painted the
figures and the flowers are
by William Billingsley.*

BELOW
*A small Derby cream jug
from a cabaret, painted
by Zachariah Boreman,
8.4 cm high, factory mark
painted in blue, c. 1790–
5. The scene is titled
underneath, 'Near
Burton, Staffordshire'.*

RIGHT
*A Derby dish from
a dessert service freely
painted with flower sprays,
22.5 cm in diameter,
factory mark in puce,
c. 1795. This dish bears
the painter's number 7
on the footrim, confirming
it was painted by William
Billingsley.*

Derby specialised in 'cabinet cups', can-shaped coffee cups and saucers that were literally intended for the display cabinet. They were, of course, far too expensive to actually use for drinking coffee. The front panel on each can was painted by one of the factory's top artists. James Banford was an accomplished figure painter. John and Robert Brewer also painted figures as well as landscapes. Other landscapes were carefully painted by Zachariah Boreman and Joseph Hill, who was known as 'Jockey Hill'. George Robertson made a speciality of shipping scenes. George Complin painted still-life subjects of fruit in baskets beside finches and other birds. The same artists also painted the centres of plates and panels on the side of fine vases, but somehow the quality of decoration on the cabinet cans surpassed everything else.

William Billingsley was one of the greatest porcelain artists of all time, for he painted flowers in a way that was different from anyone else. Indeed, his influence over all subsequent English china painters cannot be overstated. Much has been written about Billingsley's way of painting roses. To create a realistic rose, instead of building up layers of red, pink and white enamel, Billingsley applied his paint very thickly on the surface of the Derby porcelain and pushed the still wet

enamel around with his brush. The white of the porcelain glaze showed through the paint to create the lighter shades and highlights on his flowers. Billingsley didn't invent this technique, for it had been used at Meissen many years before. What makes Billingsley's brushwork different was his use of thick, wet paint that created an impressionistic effect. His flowers on Derby porcelain looked real and sold well, helping to boost the reputation of the factory. In the china shops of London customers all wanted to buy Derby's luxurious porcelain.

When John Flight arrived in Worcester in 1788 he found a sorry state of affairs. His father, Thomas Flight, had bought the porcelain factory five years before but had neglected the business until his sons were old enough to take control. The chief decorators, Humphrey and Robert Chamberlain, had left Flight's factory to set up their own rival china factory in Worcester, taking many workmen with them. The Flights were left with no experienced painters or gilders and, to make things worse, the remaining works manager was defrauding the owners. Such calamity disguised blessings, however. The Chamberlains had been set in their ways and for years had introduced little that was in any way original. To survive, Flight was forced to bring new decorators from London and this was his saving grace. Charlotte Hampton introduced to Worcester a new and brighter way of gilding fine porcelain. Taking his lead from Derby, John Flight knew he needed to take the Worcester factory up-market. He engaged John Pennington, an accomplished figure painter who was working for Wedgwood in London.

A Worcester plate from Flights' factory, painted with a figure of 'Hope' by John Pennington, 24.5 cm, special factory mark in blue, 1790–2. This important set was made for the Duke of Clarence.

Encouraged by a visit from King George III and Queen Charlotte in 1788, John Flight pursued other royal commissions and patronage. Armed with the Royal Warrant, Flights created a special set in 1790–2 for the King's brother, the Duke of Clarence, painted with figures by John Pennington. This was to be the way forward. Flights abandoned cheap blue and white and from then on only made porcelain finished off with fine gilding. Further fine painters were engaged. Samuel Smith was an enormously talented painter able to turn his hand to flowers, landscapes, birds and shells.

Wars with France did not prevent a new era of prosperity across the British Isles. New porcelain factories started to spring up like never before. Competition must have been rife – in many different sectors of the market. At the more basic level New Hall wasn't only challenged by other Staffordshire makers. Liverpool and Coalport in Shropshire were home to new factories keen to make tea sets in quantity and exploit a much-reduced supply of imported Chinese export porcelain (see pages 66–7). John Rose & Co.'s Coalport factory followed on from nearby Caughley, and like Caughley and New Hall, Coalport believed in mass production of everyday chinaware. Coalport did not completely avoid lavish decoration and ornamental productions, however, and instead John Rose became the main supplier of white porcelain 'blanks' to a new profession of independent china decorators.

The principal china dealers in London were keen to sell the latest and most fashionable styles. This meant Paris porcelain, but with the Napoleonic War in full flow, supplies were naturally unpredictable. Some richly decorated French porcelain was smuggled into Britain and by a roundabout trade dealers were able to buy a limited amount of white porcelain from Paris. This was enamelled in London with direct copies of modern French designs. One of the most influential decorating workshops in London was established in the 1790s by Thomas Baxter, a china painter from Worcester. His son, Thomas Baxter Junior, was highly talented as a porcelain decorator. Initially the Baxters painted on Paris porcelain but, with restricted supplies, the Baxter workshop turned to Coalport to provide white vases, plates and tea sets.

A Coalport vase painted with a view of the city of Rome, 30 cm high, c. 1805. Coalport supplied blank porcelain to most of the London china decorators. The gilded borders and distinctive flower painting identify this vase as from the Baxter workshop.

In 1802 the younger Thomas Baxter painted some vases with images of Lady Hamilton; these were acquired by Nelson for the home he shared with Emma Hamilton at Merton. Baxter was a society portrait painter who exhibited frequently at the Royal Academy. He visited Emma at Merton and painted special portraits of her on Coalport and Worcester porcelain. Suffering ill health, to escape the smoke of London, Baxter went to Worcester in 1814, working at Flight, Barr and Barr's china factory and in his own time he ran a china-painting school near the Cathedral. Baxter painted at Flight's factory for little more than two years, producing some of his finest work. He was an all-round 'decorator', for he also excelled at modelling and gilding. Meanwhile his pupils learnt to paint in his style.

Even before Baxter's arrival in Worcester, Flights had produced some of the most spectacular and costly porcelain available in England. Imaginative landscapes in the style known as 'Picturesque' were painted by Thomas Rogers and others. Samuel Smith and John Barker painted panels of sea shells. Realistic painted birds' feathers were scattered on the lovely white porcelain. The great William Billingsley painted flowers. The classical style gilding that finished off the porcelain was as accomplished as the painting. Flights had replaced Derby as the principal maker of rich cabinet porcelain. This was the taste of the Regency period in Britain, when the Prince of

A Flight, Barr and Barr inkstand with a simulated marble ground and painted panel of shells, 17.5 cm wide, incised B mark, c. 1800–4. Tropical sea shells were valuable objects in Regency Britain and Worcester's shell painted porcelain represented great wealth.

A Flight, Barr and Barr plate from the Stowe Service made for the Duke of Chandos, 24 cm in diameter, impressed and printed factory marks, c. 1815.

Wales acted as Regent during King George III's illness. Flights' Regency porcelain was the equivalent of the *Empire* style in France and the *Biedermeier* taste in Germany and Austria. Joseph Flight's partner, Martin Barr, is said to have encouraged the Worcester factory's decorators by continually asking them to consider the porcelain as jewellery and to take all possible pains. Only the very best craftsmanship was good enough.

To the wealthy customers, the most opulent decoration was all that mattered. Expensive porcelain didn't just mean finely painted panels. Rich 'Japan' and 'Imari' patterns decorated the best porcelain at many British china factories. Imari, in red, blue and gold, is synonymous with Derby, but similar designs were made at Coalport, Spode and Worcester. Even the mass production Staffordshire factories like New Hall all made Imari and Japan patterns. Rich colours and even richer gold was what mattered most.

Armorial porcelain no longer came from China. When the Duke of Chandos wanted a dinner set with his armorial bearings to use at his palatial home at Stowe, he wanted the very best that money could buy. He went to Flights in Worcester and the set they produced in 1814 can only be described as fantastic. If the aim was to impress his guests, the Stowe Service surpassed all belief. This was just one dinner set from one factory. All the successful

English porcelain factories made sets with coats of arms, their lavish scale limited only by the depths of customers' pockets.

Let us, just for a moment, go back in time twenty-five years earlier and consider the career of William Billingsley. In the 1780s we had left him painting flowers at Derby, but he had dreams of making his own porcelain. By 1795 he had acquired sufficient knowledge and now sought financial help in order to construct a new porcelain factory. Production began at Pinxton in 1796. Backed by John Coke, a local landowner, Billingsley's Pinxton porcelain closely resembled Derby and he decorated much of the production himself with his distinctive flowers or landscapes. The relationship between Coke and Billingsley was clearly strained and in 1799 Billingsley left the partnership, setting up a decorating workshop of his own in nearby Mansfield. Coke continued the Pinxton factory probably until 1813, but without Billingsley's painting the decoration of later Pinxton lacked excitement.

At Mansfield, William Billingsley decorated white porcelain blanks bought in from Paris, Staffordshire and Coalport. Within a few years he was making porcelain again, this time at Brampton near Torksey, a few miles away in Lincolnshire. Because Torksey porcelain was very similar to Pinxton, very little is recognised today. Neither venture was successful. Bankrupt and chased by creditors, William Billingsley fled the scene and travelling under an alias, he arrived destitute in Worcester in 1808. He was engaged as a flower painter at Flights china factory and produced some beautiful work. Once established, he assisted the potters at the Worcester factory with the construction of kilns and the development of a new kind of china body. Billingsley had his own agenda, however, and in 1813 he sneaked away from Worcester one night taking his knowledge with him to Wales. New backers financed the construction of a porcelain factory at Swansea where exciting times lay ahead.

Collectors of Welsh porcelain argue that the porcelain Billingsley created at Swansea from 1814 and subsequently at Nantgarw in South Wales is the most

A Swansea dessert dish painted by David Evans, 28.3 cm wide, red script Swansea mark, c. 1815–17. Swansea flower painting sets off the creamy-white porcelain to perfection.

A Nantgarw dish probably decorated in the London workshop of Robbins and Randall, 23 cm in diameter, impressed mark Nant-Garw CW, c. 1818–20. London decorating workshops painted Nantgarw porcelain in the latest French fashion.

beautiful ever made in Britain. Certainly this is a claim that is hard to dispute. While other makers had mostly switched to bone china recipes by this time, Billingsley's porcelain was closer to the old glassy soft paste porcelain of France. At Swansea his early 'glassy' paste was succeeded by a formula known today as 'duckegg' because of the slightly blue-tinted translucence. This was seen at its best when painted in the French taste with pretty flowers and delicate gilding. Billingsley painted some Swansea himself, and engaged other talented painters. The work of William Pollard, David Evans and Henry Morris can be distinguished by the different ways in which they painted their flowers. Thomas Baxter was persuaded to come from Worcester and while at Swansea Baxter painted very gentle local views and occasional figure subjects.

Heavy kiln failures meant success still eluded William Billingsley. For practical reasons the proprietors of the Swansea factory replaced the duckegg paste with a less delicate 'Trident' body, but meanwhile Billingsley moved on, building new kilns at Nantgarw. The new Nantgarw porcelain, probably made from 1818, was heavier and thicker than that made at Swansea and slightly creamy, but still extremely translucent. The best London decorating workshops appreciated the beauty of Nantgarw and placed orders for great quantities of white plates and cups and saucers. These were painted in London following the latest French fashions. Collectors today try to recognise the rarer 'locally decorated' Nantgarw porcelain decorated at the factory in Wales, especially flower decoration by Thomas Pardoe.

Nantgarw porcelain may have been beautiful, but it was simply too difficult to make. London decorators found supplies unreliable and were forced to switch instead to imported Paris blanks or else they used English bone china made at Coalport. Coalport made almost identical shapes to Nantgarw and when they were painted in the same London workshops, it is understandably difficult to tell some Coalport and Welsh porcelain apart.

Different proprietors continued for a few years to make porcelain at Swansea, but in 1820 production ended at Nantgarw. A large stock of undecorated Nantgarw plates remained and some of these were not painted until more than a decade later. William Billingsley is said to have walked to Coalport and he probably advised John Rose & Co. until he died near Coalport in 1828, a broken and disillusioned man. The various Welsh decorators either set up as independent china painters or joined other factories. Thomas Baxter went back to Worcester, this time joining Flights' competitors Chamberlain & Co. There old rivalries came to a head. The son of the proprietor of Chamberlain's factory, Humphrey Chamberlain Junior, was an

A Chamberlains Worcester miniature jug and basin painted with views of Worcester and Malvern, the jug 9.5 cm high, factory name marks, c. 1818–20. These are probably by Enoch Doe, while Thomas Baxter painted many similar views working at Chamberlains in his last years.

accomplished painter, responsible for superb figure painting on Chamberlains cabinet cups and vases. Thomas Baxter is reputed to have criticised Humphrey Chamberlain's painting because it was too detailed and realistic. Baxter preferred to use a stipple-painting technique to make his work more impressionistic. While working at Chamberlain's Baxter had little opportunity to paint magnificent cabinet pieces, however. His last years were spent painting endless souvenir views of Worcester and the nearby spa resort of Malvern on little trinkets aimed at tourists. He died in 1821.

Like Billingsley, Thomas Baxter also died disillusioned. Fine artist painting on English porcelain was becoming a thing of the past. It was too difficult and too costly. Customers were more interested in the overall impact of porcelain as public taste moved on during the reigns of George IV and William IV. This was to be the age of the fancy tea set.

A Swansea tureen from the 'Lysaght Service', 24 cm wide, c. 1817–20. After Billingsley's departure, the Bevington family continued the Swansea factory and engaged Henry Morris to create this sumptuous dinner service for a local family.

Chapter Six

TIME FOR TEA: 1790–1850

TEA AND FINE CHINA go hand in hand. Shipwreck cargoes recovered from the south China seas have shown that a popular folklore is true. Porcelain really did arrive in the west packed in chests of tea. Europeans loved the beverage but couldn't begin to understand accounts of the Chinese 'tea ceremony' that came with it. Instead the British developed their own ceremony of 'afternoon tea' along with many other social pastimes forged around the tea table.

The Chinese didn't use teapots. The Asian way was to add hot water from a metal kettle to leaves or powdered tea in a cup or small bowl. Brewing tea within a china teapot was the preferred European way. Some teas were sharp or bitter with a strong taste of tannin. To break this down and smooth the taste, milk was added in the teacup. Sugar, too, made tea a more pleasurable drink to European customers who found the taste unpalatable by itself. The Chinese didn't add milk or sugar to their tea and instead the merchants who brought tea from China to Europe asked the Chinese potters to create appropriate vessels for the purpose. Thus the Chinese came up with the teapot, the milk jug and the sugar bowl or *sucrier*, as it became known.

The shape of the teapot and the custom for using different shapes of cups developed in Holland, in Germany and in England. Specific orders were sent to China as fashions changed in Europe. The British preferred to drink tea from teabowls placed on saucers, while coffee was served in taller cups with handles that were placed on trays without saucers or stands. In Continental Europe in the 1740s it became the fashion to drink tea from shallow cups with handles. This Continental habit was introduced into wealthy London society during the 1750s but the middle classes continued to prefer their tea served in teabowls for several decades to come. Some sections of society even drank their tea from the saucers.

Worcester gave their customers a choice. During the 1760s and '70s tea sets of patterns in the Chinese taste were provided with teabowls, while costly European designs such as those with scale blue grounds were mostly accompanied with handled teacups. Cheaper blue and white tea sets were almost always given teabowls, for these were used by the middle classes.

By the 1780s, when the New Hall China Co. became Britain's most prolific manufacturer of tea services, they made it clear which end of the market they intended to supply. New Hall's forerunner at Bristol had made elegant teacups copied from Meissen. In Staffordshire they mass-produced teabowls instead. Initially these were quite small, but as tea became cheaper towards the end of the eighteenth century, New Hall teabowls were made in larger sizes. By this date the British tea service was made up of standard components. As the teapot was to be filled with hot tea, it was provided with a matching porcelain teapot stand. The sugar box or *sucrier* normally had a cover to protect the costly contents from flies. A small jug could be used for milk or cream. Instead of cakes or biscuits, in the eighteenth century tea was served with slices of bread and butter. A single 'bread and butter plate' was used and passed round among the guests. By the nineteenth century two plates became the fashion, one usually a bit larger than the other. Tea services also included a bowl known as a 'slop bowl' or 'waste bowl': the dregs from the cups were poured into it before refilling.

Most tea services came with twelve cups and saucers, although smaller sets for six were not unusual. Normally the sets also came with twelve coffee cups, but these didn't have their own saucers. Because you never served coffee and tea at the same time, it was customary for the cups to share the same saucer. Thus a full set contained twelve teacups or teabowls, twelve coffee cups and twelve saucers. Strangely, though, coffee pots were very much luxury items and in Britain coffee pots were purchased separately. Families used a treasured silver coffee pot that became something of an heirloom. English porcelain coffee pots are very much rarer than teapots, a tradition that came from China as Chinese coffee pots are likewise just as scarce.

In the china shops of Britain, New Hall tea sets competed directly with cheaper imported Chinese tea services. The price of the Chinese teawares had fallen and this annoyed the dealers whose profits fell. To earn more, the dealers got together and formed 'rings' at the London auctions where the Chinese porcelain was sold, artificially rigging the prices to buy the imported china as cheaply as possible. The East India Company decided to take action and to teach the dealers a lesson; the

A New Hall tea service of spiral-fluted shape popular around 1800. The pattern is in French taste but this set still contains Chinese-type teabowls. The coffee cups and teabowls share the same saucers.

A Miles Mason teapot decorated with the popular 'Boy in a Doorway' pattern, c. 1805–8. In his factory in Staffordshire Mason reproduced the kind of porcelain he had previously imported as a dealer in Chinese porcelain.

company reduced and eventually suspended the bulk import of porcelain into Britain. This left the way clear for china makers in Staffordshire to expand their own trade enormously. Many new factories started up in the years either side of 1800. Miles Mason had been a dealer in Chinese porcelain and was probably one of the people who had rigged the London auctions. Unable to obtain Chinese porcelain any more, he switched to manufacture and started a factory in Staffordshire making tea services and plates and dishes that looked exactly like the ones he used to import.

The Chinese had meticulously hand painted their blue and white teawares. Miles Mason followed the traditions of Worcester and Caughley and used transfer printing in underglaze blue because it was simpler and cheaper. Making a profit out of porcelain manufacture was all about price and understanding your marketplace. Some makers supplied the cheaper end of the market while some of these same makers aimed other products at the middle market too. There was also a luxury end of the market where wealthy families could afford the best china tea sets money could buy. The wide choice that was available in the early nineteenth century provides enormous scope to porcelain collectors two centuries later.

One frustrating thing about collecting nineteenth-century British porcelain is the serious shortage of marked specimens. Hardly any teaware or tableware includes the maker's name underneath. The reason for this lies with the china shops of the time. Few porcelain manufacturers sold directly to the public and instead customers bought their tea sets from china shops. The china dealers wanted to keep their business and didn't want customers contacting the manufacturers if they wanted replacements or additions. Therefore the dealers would not allow makers to put their names on their porcelain. As a general rule, only those factories that operated their own retail shops put their names on their china as a factory mark. The great majority didn't mark their porcelain. The largest of all the English porcelain makers at the time was John Rose & Co. at Coalport and yet this important factory marked its name on only the tiniest proportion of its products.

To confuse collectors even more, everyone copied everybody else. To begin with, all of the English factories copied their shapes and patterns from the Chinese. As tastes and fashions changed, as soon as one maker produced a range of tableware that sold well, the china dealers asked other factories to make the same shapes and patterns. Patents and copyrights were costly to obtain and almost impossible to enforce. Successful china factories had to make fashionable tea sets and if this meant copying somebody else's idea, then so be it. Different factories gave their own names to their various teaware shapes. The Spode factory's records survive and we know that their most popular teaware range around 1815–20 was called the 'London' shape. Teapot collectors today use the Spode name to identify this shape, but it has to be remembered that dozens of other china makers also produced this popular shape at the same time. Recognising one factory's London shape from another requires extensive detective work. The angle and thickness of the handles varies and different makers used different sequences of pattern numbers. These clues help – the Swansea version is very thin and sharply pointed, for example – but for every London shape tea set that can be identified, twenty others remain anonymous.

A number of specialised books are available to help collectors identify the products and shapes of different china factories. A huge number of firms made porcelain tea services in Britain during the period from 1820–50. These were popularly given as wedding presents and were looked after lovingly. As a result a surprising number of sets survives today and many are extraordinarily good value. Collectors have to be selective as full tea services take up a lot of room. It is usual for collectors to specialise, in either a single shape or maker. You can collect all different shapes and designs made by Davenport, or Spode, or Daniel, for example, using a standard reference book about the factory as your 'collectors' Bible'. Alternatively you can collect just teapots from lots of different makers – or cups and saucers – or milk jugs.

Some factories are traditionally more collectable and expensive than others. Because of their high quality, the Welsh factories of Swansea and Nantgarw have a very strong following, particularly from collectors living in South Wales today. Derby and Pinxton likewise have a strong local following, whereas the many Staffordshire china factories have attracted far fewer collectors in proportion to their size. There was only one major porcelain factory in Yorkshire in northern Britain and as a result the Rockingham China Works at Swinton on the Marquis of Rockingham's estate has become almost legendary. Rockingham porcelain can be very fine and so deserves the attention of collectors, but of the great English china factories, Rockingham is by far the most

misunderstood. This is surprising as Rockingham is one of the few factories that regularly marked its chinaware. Proud to have been awarded the Royal Warrant by William IV in 1830, the factory marked its plates and saucers with the Rockingham family name and crest of a griffin, with the slogan 'Manufacturers to the King'. The form of the mark is a guide to dating, as after Victoria's coronation in 1837 the mark changed to 'Rockingham Works… Manufacturers to the Queen'.

A Davenport teapot of extraordinary shape entwined with branches of simulated coral, 15 cm high, printed factory mark, c. 1830–7. This was probably intended for a china cabinet rather than as a teapot to use.

A Rockingham tureen for sugar or cream from a dessert service, 19.8 cm wide, printed factory mark in purple, c. 1830–5. The shape with a high foot combined with scroll and shell handles is unique to the Rockingham factory.

A Mintons 'Dresden vase' painted with Watteau-style figures and with a figurine forming the finial, 43 cm high, c. 1835. This is typical of the 'English Dresden' taste copied from contemporary Meissen.

With so many marked pieces the study of Rockingham ought to have been easy, but instead confusion abounds. Simply because Rockingham marked its tea sets and they looked very similar to everyone else's, collectors a hundred years ago wrongly assumed that all the other unmarked tea sets were also made at Rockingham. A simple mistake perhaps, but it meant that every family in Britain believed they had inherited a Rockingham tea set.

Research by Geoffrey Godden and other experts during the 1960s and '70s sorted out the mess and a new generation of British porcelain collectors began to look at the evidence. They noticed how fashions changed during successive decades of the nineteenth century. Relatively plain shapes popular during the Regency period – represented by the 'London' shape – were replaced by ever-more complicated and fussy shapes during the 1820s and '30s. By the time of Queen Victoria's reign the rococo revival was in full swing. The influences were almost all from Continental Europe, initially from France and then from Germany. A new term was coined to describe this fashion. 'English Dresden' was Britain's answer to imported Meissen porcelain.

During the 1830s and early '40s, the Meissen factory near Dresden was exporting huge amounts of high-quality porcelain to Britain. Indeed, London was Meissen's most important marketplace. At this date Meissen was revisiting the designs it had made eighty years earlier when rococo was the height of fashion. Classical elegance had all but replaced rococo but by the 1830s customers were tired of straight lines and fashion demanded something more frivolous once again. Rococo designs were back in fashion in Paris also, so it was inevitable that in Britain public taste would change too, especially with the arrival of a new young Queen.

Vases and ornaments reflecting the 'English Dresden' taste were smothered with rococo scrollwork and flowers – painted flowers, tiny modelled flowers or entire vessels in the shape of plants and flora. Tea sets were redesigned to reflect this new mood. Every inch was covered with decoration. Surprisingly the most popular coloured grounds were not as vibrant as some of the Regency excesses. Pale yellow or fawn and drab grey were the most favoured backgrounds while deep blue mixed with pale yellow was also popular. Simple flowers or birds, or imaginary landscape vignettes were painted into the reserved panels, which were irregularly shaped and framed with fancy gilding.

A Coalport vase in the 'Coalbrookdale' style, c. 1840. The original owner would have sprinkled perfume on the china flowers to create a form of air freshener.

Hand in hand with this new taste in teawares, the Coalport factory, which was Britain's biggest and most influential china maker, created 'Coalbrookdale'. Curiously named after the local iron-casting works, this topical style of porcelain decoration was decidedly frivolous. The word 'taste' is hard to apply to these wares objectively, for they were decidedly over-the-top. Modelled china flowers were stuck onto the surface of elaborate ornamental shapes and coloured to look like real flowers and leaves. The fashion for flower-encrusted porcelain was copied from the Continent and many Coalbrookdale objects were direct reproductions of Meissen. Coalport was not the only maker to take this 'English Dresden' style in hand. Most English china factories had a go, especially Mintons and Alcocks, while even Derby, Rockingham and the Worcester factories of Chamberlains and Graingers made their versions of flower-encrusted porcelain. Many of these English rococo porcelains were marked underneath with copies of Meissen's crossed swords mark and understandably they confuse collectors today. Nowadays the name 'Coalbrookdale' is used generically. Technically this should apply only to Dresden styles made at Coalport, but the products of most makers look alike.

Alongside Dresden-style ornamental porcelain and tea services, the other staple product of English porcelain factories in the nineteenth century remained the dessert service. The dessert course was just as important in Victorian times as it had been a century before, giving well-to-do families the chance to show off their best

A Davenport dessert service, each piece with a different fruit specimen, painted with botanical accuracy, printed marks, c. 1845. Victorians considered fruit a very appropriate decoration for dessert services.

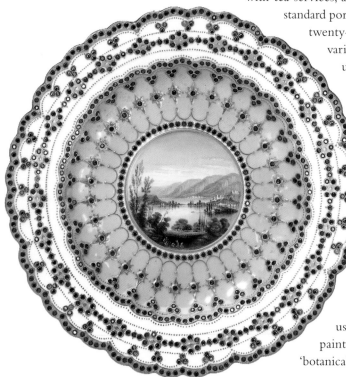

chinaware. Fruit remained expensive and sugar and cream were even more so. In middle-class homes a separate set of plates and dishes was used to serve dessert. As with tea services, a set number of components made up a standard porcelain dessert service. Twelve, eighteen or twenty-four plates were accompanied by variously shaped dishes. A complete set was usually provided with a pair of each of four different shapes of serving dish. One much larger dish raised up on a high foot formed what was known as the centrepiece.

During the second half of the nineteenth century new fashions called for major changes to standard porcelain services. After 1850–60, dessert services now came with fruit stands known as 'comports' raising the dishes up on spreading stems of differing heights. They became taller and narrower as the nineteenth century progressed. It was usual for each plate or comport to be painted with a different subject. Realistic 'botanical' flower specimens were popular, as well as different birds which were recognisable species, each named on the back of the plates. Landscape views were likewise copied from travel books and the name of the view was painted on the back of the plate. Dessert services provided subjects of conversation at smart dinner parties as well as a chance for their owners to show off.

A more dramatic change occurred with tea services. In the 1840s in America tea became much cheaper and it became quite acceptable even in fashionable society to drink tea from the saucer. American china shops sold imported British tea sets with a new kind of little plate called a 'cup plate'. As the name suggests, ladies would place their cup on the cup plate while they drank from the saucer. American glass manufacturers made glass cup plates to sell to families whose old tea sets did not come with these tiny plates.

In smarter sections of society, drinking from the saucer was still frowned upon. By the 1850s arguments frequently broke out over the tea table. To discourage the habit of drinking from the saucer, china manufacturers were asked to make saucers with sunken wells – central depressions which would fit the shape of the cup – indicating that the saucer was there as something on which to stand your cup and not as an item for drinking out of. A bigger version of a cup plate was now provided with these re-designed tea services. This became the 'side plate', which was ideal for a single sandwich, cake or biscuit.

To sum up, tea services with plain saucers without moulded wells in the centres are likely to be before 1850 in date and will not have matching side plates. The fashion for side plates, or teaplates as they became known, was only slowly adopted and so generally these will indicate a date after 1860. Meanwhile, dessert services with comports instead of flat dishes will also be from the second half of the nineteenth century and are rarely found before 1865.

Queen Victoria wanted a tea set to use at her Scottish castle at Balmoral, and Mintons designed an appropriate border based on Prince Albert's tartan. The set was made in 1890 and so by this date the saucers were made with central wells to hold the cups.

Chapter Seven

VICTORIAN MAGNIFICENCE: 1851–1901

Tʜᴇ ɢʀᴇᴀᴛ ᴇxʜɪʙɪᴛɪᴏɴ in Hyde Park was more than just a giant shop window for British industry. It was a place to see and be seen. It was a chance for Britain's porcelain makers to show off their latest products and innovations, but equally it gave them an opportunity to learn from their competitors. Looking back on this extraordinary event, it is just as interesting to note what was not on display. There was no Derby porcelain, for example, as the once great Derby factory had closed in 1848. A new manufactory had been established in a separate part of Derby, but was in no position to show at the 1851 Exhibition. Worcester was represented in Hyde Park by Chamberlain & Co. who put on a pathetic display of past glories from their museum collection with just a handful of new porcelain pieces copied from Sèvres. John Rose & Co. of Coalport made a respectable effort, but in terms of British porcelain makers most of the praise from the critics and judges at the Great Exhibition went to just two makers, Copelands and Mintons, who both showed an important new kind of British porcelain.

Parian was 'statuary porcelain', a special version of bone china with added glass that could simulate carved marble without the need for a separate layer of glaze to keep it clean. Named after the finest source of white marble in Roman times, parian enabled fine art statues and busts to be manufactured commercially and this innovation led to a revival of interest in porcelain figures. Since Derby's decline, porcelain figure making had been disappointing in Britain. The Worcester factories, Rockingham and Mintons made a few figures but these struggled to compete with masses of imported Meissen figures. Mostly it was left to pottery makers in Staffordshire to produce figural ornaments. Some Staffordshire figures such as images of Queen Victoria and Prince Albert were made from bone china but these were comical representations, not fine portraits. In 1839 the young Queen Victoria went twice to see a handsome American lion tamer, Isaac van Amburgh, at Drury Lane theatre. His portrait in Staffordshire porcelain is pure folk art and worlds apart from the parian figures shown at the Great Exhibition.

The glowing press reviews Mintons received at the Great Exhibition were well deserved, but the factory had influential help. Herbert Minton's friend and advisor, Henry Cole, was a close acquaintance of the Prince Consort and one of the main guiding forces behind the Exhibition. Portraits of Queen Victoria and Prince Albert were made in Mintons parian. What made these different from most previous British porcelain figures was the use by Mintons of freelance sculptors, some of the most eminent modellers of the day. Both Copelands and Mintons bought the rights to

OPPOSITE
A massive Mintons floor vase with 'cloisonné' decoration, showing the design influence of Dr Christopher Dresser, 60 cm high, c. 1880

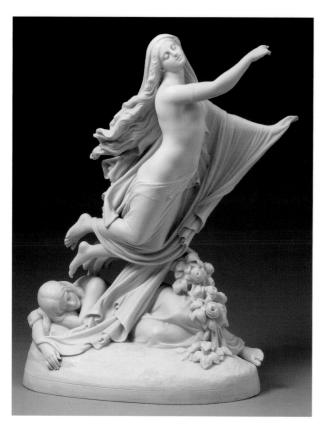

ABOVE *'The Sleep of Sorrow and the Dream of Joy' by the eminent sculptor Raphaelle Monti was reproduced in a more manageable size in parian by Copelands. Published by the Crystal Palace Art Union in 1874, the Copeland version is still an impressive 48.5 cm high.*

ABOVE *An English parian figure of the 'Greek Slave', copied from Hiram Powers' marble statue that caused a sensation at the Great Exhibition. This example from c. 1855 is unmarked but Mintons also made a version in parian.*

LEFT *When Queen Victoria went to see American lion tamer Isaac van Amburgh in 1839 she commissioned his portrait in oils. Other visitors to his shows could buy a souvenir figure comically rendered in Staffordshire porcelain, 16.5 cm high.*

make scaled-down versions of the most famous statues exhibited by the world's leading sculptors. Huge queues formed to view Hiram Powers' controversial marble statue the 'Greek Slave' when it was shown at the 1851 exhibition. Mintons soon produced a portable version in parian, ideal for a gentlemen to place in his library or the parlour of his respectable home where a naked beauty could be displayed in the name of art.

Inside the splendid exhibition halls, plain white parian was in complete contrast to the rest of Mintons' display. Their colourful Majolica reflected the more outrageous side of Victorian taste, but as this was a new form of pottery it falls outside the scope of this book. Also on show was some of the most splendid and sumptuous porcelain. Queen Victoria spent a long time viewing Mintons' massive stand at the Great Exhibition. Their new Sèvres-style porcelain impressed the Queen more than anything and she ordered a magnificent dessert service with a similar rich turquoise ground. Herbert Minton knew that some of the wealthiest homes in Britain contained collections of eighteenth-century Sèvres and he had arranged to borrow priceless specimens for his factory's craftsmen to copy. They did an excellent job and Mintons' reproductions of old Sèvres vases really do look the part.

Mintons' triumph at the 1851 Exhibition gave other British porcelain makers a fresh impetus and the desire to catch up. The ailing Worcester porcelain company

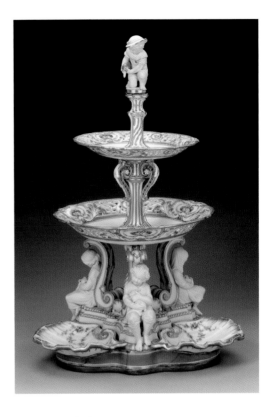

ABOVE
A duplicate centrepiece from the Mintons dessert service ordered by Queen Victoria after viewing Mintons' display at the Great Exhibition. The Queen was fond of the turquoise colour, combined with white parian.

LEFT
A pair of Mintons elephant-handled vases made as exact reproductions of early Sèvres, 30 cm high, dated 1876. Mintons borrowed priceless specimens of eighteenth-century Sèvres for their craftsmen to copy.

BELOW

Thomas Bott invented the 'Worcester Enamels' copied from old Limoges enamel. His son, Thomas Bott Jr, took the technique to rival manufacturers, in this case Brown-Westhead, Moore & Co. where this vase was made c. 1890, 50 cm high, marked 'Cauldon Ware'.

BELOW RIGHT
When Kerr and Binns of Worcester created the Raphael Plateau as a bridal presentation in 1854, they had only just discovered the new material called parian. Worcester's best artist, Thomas Bott, painted the story of Cupid and Psyche in a series of panels. 46 cm diameter.

sought new backing, both financial and artistic, and engaged two new directors with retail backgrounds. W. H. Kerr was a prominent china dealer in Dublin while Richard Binns worked for the largest glass-seller in London. From 1852 the Worcester partnership of Kerr and Binns completely transformed china making in the city. They introduced parian and in order to compete with Mintons and Copelands, Kerr and Binns realised the necessity of using freelance modellers. At the Dublin Exhibition in 1853 Worcester's 'Shakespeare Dessert Service' combined fine painting and gilding with Parian figures created by a young Irish sculptor named William Boyton Kirk. Queen Victoria was greatly impressed and Prince Albert now took notice of the Worcester factory.

The Prince Consort invited R. W. Binns to visit Buckingham Palace and show him specimens of a new invention called 'Worcester Enamels'. A talented glass painter, Thomas Bott was Mr Binns' protégé. Bott had discovered how to reproduce medieval Limoges enamels using English bone china. On top of a deep blue glaze, Bott built up many layers of opaque white enamel. Prince Albert allowed Thomas Bott to examine priceless Limoges enamels in the Royal Collection, and he encouraged the Queen to order a Worcester dessert service in the Limoges enamel technique but using Queen Victoria's favourite turquoise colour instead of deep blue. True to the taste of the time, this was also combined with parian figures supporting the comports and centerpieces.

Spurred on by royal patronage, the former partnership of Kerr and Binns was now known as the Worcester Royal Porcelain Company. Thomas Bott's copies of Limoges enamel caused a sensation at the 1862 Exhibition in London and R. W. Binns knew that he had truly arrived on the world stage when even the great Meissen factory made what they

called 'Worcester Ware'. Coalport and Mintons also made imitations of Worcester's Limoges enamel decoration. Copying was considered fair game in the porcelain industry. Taking his lead from Mintons, Mr Binns introduced Majolica and he also engaged a French artist, Charles Palmere, to paint Sèvres-style decoration at Worcester. Commercially, though, most of these copied techniques turned out to be failures.

Mintons saw France as the past and the future. Looking ahead, they engaged as Art Director a highly experienced French ceramicist who had worked at Sèvres. Leon Arnoux brought with him knowledge and important contacts, encouraging many senior French artists and designers to leave Paris for Stoke-on-Trent. Skilled china painters included Antonin and Lucien Boullemier and Désiré Leroy. Foremost among the French decorators employed at Mintons was Louis Solon who excelled at a new technique called *pâte-sur-pâte*. Literally translated as 'clay-on-clay', this involved building up depths of textured white clay on top of a dark coloured background. Finely tooled and fired in the kiln, the effect is completed by a separate covering of glaze. The decoration is translucent and delicate, sealed for all time beneath a protective layer of glass. In Solon's skilled hands depth and perspective shine out in three dimensions, the diaphanous skirts of his maidens leaving little to the imagination.

Solon began work at Mintons in 1870 and soon built up a major department where he trained pupils and assistants. Mintons may not have invented *pâte-sur-pâte* but owing to the leadership of Louis Solon, his name and the name of Mintons will forever be synonymous with this technique. His important vases now featured in every international exhibition. His artistry was technically superb, if perhaps of questionable morality by today's standards. He drew heavily on images of maidens and Cupids, representing the battle for

A massive Copelands vase signed by C.F. Hürten, 68 cm high, c. 1865. Copelands engaged this very talented artist from Germany to paint flowers in the European manner. Hürten had learnt painting on Berlin plaques but he couldn't achieve quite the same detail on Staffordshire bone china. Even so, by British standards his work is outstanding.

A Mintons moon vase decorated by Leon Arnoux, the firm's Art Director. 28 cm high, c. 1878. Arnoux encouraged many other French ceramic artists to join him at Stoke-on-Trent.

ABOVE
'Butterflies', an incredible Mintons vase with pâte-sur-pâte decoration by Louis Solon. 32.1 cm high. Made in 1900, records show that Solon worked on this vase for twenty days. Louis Solon was by far the greatest exponent of this difficult technique.

ABOVE RIGHT
A Royal Worcester vase made as an exact copy of a Japanese ivory original, 26.5 cm high, puce factory mark, dated 1872. This model was shown at the Vienna Exhibition in 1872 when Worcester launched its new 'Japanesque' porcelain.

love. Solon's love is more often lost than found, rivalry and jealousy fighting for attention with an emphasis on punishment and chastisement fuelled with more than their fair share of whips, cages and chains.

Louis Solon's art was ahead of its time, anticipating the spirit of art nouveau. Privately he studied and collected old pottery and porcelain and wrote pioneering books helping to record the early history of the ceramics industry in Staffordshire before it was forgotten. R.W. Binns at Worcester likewise studied the history of porcelain and preserved his factory's own collection of reference pieces. Binns was an obsessive collector of a very different kind of art. When Japan re-opened its doors to international trade after a century of self-imposed isolation, its arts and crafts caused a sensation in the West. At exhibitions in 1862 and 1867 Binns was a major buyer of the best Japanese art, especially ceramics. He constructed his own museum of Japanese art at the Royal Worcester factory in order to inspire his own craftsmen. Binns used the Vienna Exhibition in 1872 as the platform to launch Worcester's 'Japanesque' porcelain. Some models were directly copied from objects in Binns' collection. Others were adaptations, combining decorative motifs from Japan and China brought together in a curious harmony.

Critics raved about Worcester's 'ivory porcelain'. Thanks to the skilful gilders and enamellers at Worcester, their figures and vases were coloured in perfect imitation of Japanese lacquer, bronze and old carved ivory. The Callowhill Brothers, Thomas and James, excelled in tooled goldwork, while a Frenchman, Edouard Béjot, was able to match any colour and texture, adding metallic shades and raised enamel jewels. The result was even more remarkable because Worcester's principal factory modeller, James Hadley, could style the faces of his figures with perfect oriental expressions. His museum collection helped, but Binns went a stage further, bringing to Worcester an actual china painter from Canton named Po Hing. Royal Worcester plates painted by a real Chinaman were certainly a novelty in 1875.

The craze for all things oriental swept through other porcelain factories in Britain. Mintons engaged an extraordinarily innovative designer, Dr Christopher Dresser, to help them create their own versions of 'Japanesque' and Chinese style porcelain. Dresser was attracted to the pure colours and clean lines of oriental *cloisonné* enamel and he helped Mintons to develop their own range of *cloisonné*-style porcelain. Only a few of Mintons' oriental designs can be attributed with certainty to Dr Dresser, for he was very influential and had many followers. Dresser was part of what became known as the 'Aesthetic Movement' in British art. This was the height of fashion in the early 1880s, synonymous with Oscar Wilde and caricatured by Gilbert and Sullivan

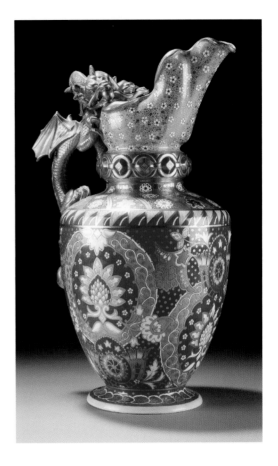

A Copelands ewer in the 'Aesthetic' taste, 38 cm high, c. 1880. The Aesthetic Movement in British art created some very elegant porcelain and plenty that reached other extremes.

in their comic operetta *Patience*. Royal Worcester created the 'Aesthetic Teapot' as a satirical comment in porcelain. Part of the humour hidden in Worcester's novelty teapot poked fun at collectors' obsession with oriental art, in particular a supposedly perfect oriental teapot that was exhibited at the Grosvenor Gallery in London. A single, plain teapot from China was said to be the complete antithesis of the excessive, over-decorated art that was seen everywhere in Victorian Britain.

Worcester's 'Aesthetic Teapot' was modelled by James Hadley, who was very much part of the establishment responsible for creating the most elaborate excesses in English ceramics. As a sculptor, Hadley could model in any style the public wanted. Unlike Mintons, Royal Worcester was not committed to plain white parian and instead James Hadley's figures were intended to be fully decorated. Many imitated the figures made of ivory and painted bronze popularly imported from Vienna. Exotic subjects ranged from Greek maidens, African warriors and Indian craftsmen to people from the nomadic tribes of the Middle East. Closer to home James Hadley depicted the children of Britain as well-behaved schoolboys and girls inspired by the prim and proper book illustrations of Kate Greenaway.

Hadley's Worcester figures were the up-market versions of the cheap Staffordshire pottery chimney ornaments and the pretty candlestick figures imported from Dresden. Hadley's pupil at Worcester, Charles Noke, introduced similar styles of

A pair of Royal Worcester figures of Moorish slaves modelled by James Hadley, 61 cm high, factory marks dated 1895. A most versatile sculptor, Hadley created many monumental figures that hardly look like porcelain at all.

A Belleek porcelain shell-shaped bowl raised on a base of coral, 17 cm, First Period mark, c. 1880. This shape was intended as a sugar bowl but, made with eggshell thinness, it could never survive much actual use.

figures at Doultons. Rivals in Staffordshire such as Copelands and a new factory run by the Moore Brothers copied the Dresden style but they preferred to leave their figure models predominantly white or finished off with simple gilding. At Belleek in Northern Ireland plain white glazed porcelain was reinvented. Belleek's parian body was given a warm creamy glaze and a gentle mother-of-pearl iridescent sheen that resembled sea shells. Belleek made relatively few figures but specialised instead in tea sets, often of eggshell thinness and shaped like real sea shells.

Belleek's delicate white tea sets competed in the china shops of Britain with Royal Worcester's imitation ivory porcelain. Old Derby Japan patterns revived at Royal Crown Derby sold alongside new Imari wares and Noritake eggshell coffee sets shipped in quantity from Japan. Customers could also choose floral tea sets imported from Dresden and a new style of popular porcelain decoration that flooded into Britain from Limoges. French porcelain factories in Limoges specialised in tea sets and dessert services with irregular scrolling rims shaded in subtle colours with a dusting of gold.

This was the taste of the 1890s right across Europe. Royal Worcester was a market leader and yet potters at Worcester also copied Limoges. A short-lived porcelain factory in Glasgow epitomises British ceramics at the time. Nautilus porcelain doesn't look remotely Scottish, for it copied designs from Belleek, Worcester and above all Limoges. Wheels had turned full circle and rococo was back in vogue in Britain just as it had been in the 1750s and the 1830s. The simplicity of form advocated by Christopher Dresser had failed to catch on. All of Europe was in need of a taste change, but while art nouveau was still just around the corner, Queen Victoria's Diamond Jubilee was celebrated with complicated and mixed up styles. Coalport's Jubilee vase of 1897 and Royal Worcester's Imperial vase of 1900 both sum it all up. Every inch of these vases was covered with decoration and somehow they found room to squeeze in some more. These vases celebrated the British Empire and they were bought by customers in far away Australia and New Zealand, India, Canada and South Africa. British porcelain was proudly exported around the globe.

BELOW LEFT
A Nautilus porcelain vase with hand-painted flowers, 21 cm high, printed marks, c. 1895. This was made in Glasgow in the style of contemporary Limoges porcelain.

BELOW
The Coalport Jubilee vase of 1897, a special limited edition celebrating all the achievements of Queen Victoria's reign. This impressive creation epitomises British taste as the nineteenth century came to a close.

Chapter Eight

DESIGN AND
TRADITION: 1900–70

THE Exposition Universelle held in Paris in 1900 marked a great watershed, but in British porcelain change did not happen overnight. A series of French terms are used for the extremes of popular fashion. *Fin de siècle* and *belle époque* sum up popular taste from the 1890s and leading up to the First World War. For those with money, the 1890s were a period of decadence and opulence which all art manufacturers were keen to exploit. Whether in the architecture of their homes or the decoration of their tea sets, customers wanted to show they had got their money's worth. If porcelain was expensive, it had to look expensive and that meant a lot of lavish ornament.

British displays at the Chicago Exhibition seven years before Paris reveal why change was inevitable. All of the major porcelain factories had created special exhibition vases to make their displays stand out. Royal Worcester's 'Chicago Vase' stood an incredible 4 feet 6 inches high. James Hadley had modelled cherubs to float among the ivory and shaded gold scrollwork of the handles and foot, while the massive body was painted with flowers by Edward Raby. It needed the construction of a new kiln at Worcester just to fire it. It was an incredible technical achievement, but artistically it was decidedly old-fashioned.

Art nouveau was, as the name suggests, something new and refreshing. The term derives from the name of a gallery opened in Paris in 1895 by an art dealer named Siegfried Bing. The Art Nouveau pavilion at the Paris Exhibition in 1900 was a sensation, inspiring many of the fifty million visitors. The principal inspiration for art nouveau came from nature. In the natural world most plant forms are curvilinear, free from straight lines and with no right angles. Art nouveau was a reaction against the over-decorated architecture-led styles of the nineteenth century. The 'new art' was extraordinarily different.

One young English visitor to the Exposition Universelle was John Wadsworth, a student at the Royal College of Art. While he was studying design at South Kensington in 1902 he met Leon Solon, the son of the Mintons' *pâte-sur-pâte* artist Louis Solon. Leon Solon was looking for an assistant Art Director to help introduce new designs at the Mintons factory. Impressed with Wadsworth's work, he promoted him to Art Director in 1905. John Wadsworth had kept a keen eye on modern art and design in Paris and in particular he was aware of the art nouveau porcelain being made at Sèvres. Wadsworth brought radical new ideas to Stoke-on-Trent. From Vienna came the inspiration for Secessionist ware combining traditional Majolica glazes with up-to-date Continental art nouveau patterns. These were mostly made in earthenware but Wadsworth was also keen to modernise Mintons' porcelain production.

OPPOSITE
A collection of original tableware designs by John Wadsworth, produced in the 1930s when he was a freelance designer in Stoke-on-Trent.

RIGHT *A Mintons vase made in 1925, 16.8 cm wide, using a shape designed by John Wadsworth in 1908. Wadsworth brought radical art nouveau designs to Mintons, but the decoration they applied, in this case* pâte-sur-pâte *by Alboin Birks, was often old fashioned.*

BELOW *A pair of Royal Doulton 'Titanian' vases painted by Harry Allen, 25.5 cm high, c. 1920. With Allen's artistry and Doultons' skilful control of chemicals and glazes, some incredible modern effects were created.*

BELOW RIGHT
A Royal Doulton 'Sung' vase painted by Charles Noke and with a 'Flambé' glaze, 24 cm high, c. 1925. Noke was a brilliant ceramicist and he helped Doultons develop some remarkable glazes.

A series of small china vases was introduced at Mintons around 1906–8. The shapes were refreshingly modern but the decoration was mostly a compromise. Painted flower panels were placed among coloured grounds finished off with raised gilding. Others used *pâte-sur-pâte*, now made commercially using moulded techniques. The influence was Sèvres from the eighteenth and nineteenth centuries, not art nouveau, and the vases fell between stools. Traditional Mintons customers

didn't buy them and the vases were not brave or exciting enough to appeal to avant-garde china buyers in Britain. Mintons' Secessionist earthenware sold very well, but their art nouveau porcelain is extremely scarce today, an indication that customers didn't buy them at the time.

The same thing happened at Royal Worcester. In 1905 a small number of very high quality porcelain vases were made using art nouveau designs but hardly any sold. They were finished off using very intricate raised gilding and this made the vases expensive. The gilding also compromised the purity of the organic plant designs. A number of Worcester's art nouveau vases survive in the factory museum for they could not find buyers at the time. English art nouveau porcelain is surprisingly hard to find.

In Britain it was left to 'art pottery' manufacturers to lead the way into the modern ceramics world. Only one British porcelain factory really succeeded with art nouveau porcelain and this was as a sideline. Royal Doulton was Britain's leading art pottery maker. After 1900 chemists at Doultons worked to develop new glaze effects that could be used on bone china. The results they achieved with their 'Titanian', 'Sung' and 'Flambé' ranges were quite remarkable. The most curious effects were created when decoration painted in underglaze colours was viewed through translucent coloured glazes. The geniuses behind these wares were Charles Noke and Harry Nixon. Noke had come a long way since he learnt modelling working with James Hadley at Worcester. At Doultons, Noke and Nixon aimed to reproduce the innovative high-temperature art porcelain made at European factories like Royal Copenhagen and Meissen. It was much harder to achieve the same effects in English bone china. Royal Worcester had tried the same thing with their art porcelain, which they called 'Sabrina Ware'. Very occasionally Worcester succeeded, but most Sabrina Ware does not come near to the beauty of Doultons' Titanian ware. At its best, Doultons' Flambé is the finest red-glazed porcelain made in Europe.

There is a perfectly good reason why English porcelain makers were slow to adapt to the new fashions from Paris and Vienna. Mostly they were selling everyday tea sets and tableware to customers who were happy with old-fashioned porcelain. More costly ornamental porcelain was likewise bought by families who lived in traditional British homes and they were not ready for art nouveau. They still bought the same 'Blush Ivory' Royal Worcester porcelain that had been made for twenty years and this was still selling well another twenty years later. In the 1920s when Clarice Cliff's art deco was all the rage, Royal Worcester still sold tableware patterns popular forty years earlier. Royal Crown Derby is known for its Imari patterns, some of which are still made today, nearly two hundred years after their introduction. This makes a mockery of changing tastes and fashions. Some traditions just keep on selling, outlasting generations.

Thus, while modern designs were filling the pages of *The Studio* magazine, the most popular tableware sold in Edwardian Britain was

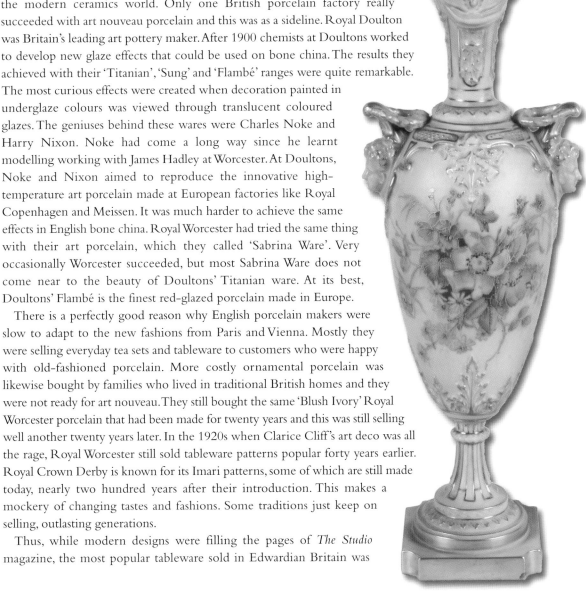

A Royal Worcester vase with a shaded background known as 'Blush Ivory', 28 cm high, dated 1917. By this date, while the rest of Europe had embraced art nouveau, most British porcelain makers remained staunchly traditional.

ABOVE
A Royal Crown Derby dinner service of the so-called 'Cigar' pattern. This one was made in the 1970s yet it could easily have been made a hundred years ago. British china buyers are old fashioned and some Royal Crown Derby Imari patterns are still made today, two hundred years after their introduction.

LEFT
A Royal Crown Derby plate from the Judge Gary Service made in 1909, the painting signed by both Cuthbert Gresley and Albert Gregory, with gilding signed by Albert Darlington, 23 cm in diameter. This plate would only be used for the fish course.

Blue Willow, a pattern that was already a hundred years old. Chinese blue and white porcelain was still being made and was being imported into Britain in quantities. Japanese porcelain, too, was sold in china shops all over Britain. Much of this was decorated in the Imari taste, enamelled and gilded in red, blue and gold. This style and colouring had been popular in Regency England (see page 60) and now enjoyed a revival thanks to Royal Crown Derby. It certainly wasn't modern, but it kept the Derby factory going during difficult times in the 1920s.

The decades following the First World War were tough for the British porcelain industry. Many firms in the Potteries closed. Cheap tableware from Bohemia (Czechoslovakia) and even Japan undercut British production and customers didn't care that the imported wares were printed with coloured photographs and lithographic transfers. The best British firms like Mintons, Copelands, and Royal Worcester were able to produce hand-decorated tableware at a price, but during years of depression luxury struggled to find a market. There was still wealth around, but it was mostly in the New World rather than the old countries.

American industrialists were the new equivalent of the British titled aristocracy. In 1909 Royal Crown Derby and Minton both made extensive services for Judge E. H. Gary, a wealthy New York millionaire who had founded the United Steel Corporation. Money was no object and the Gary Service was the most costly set

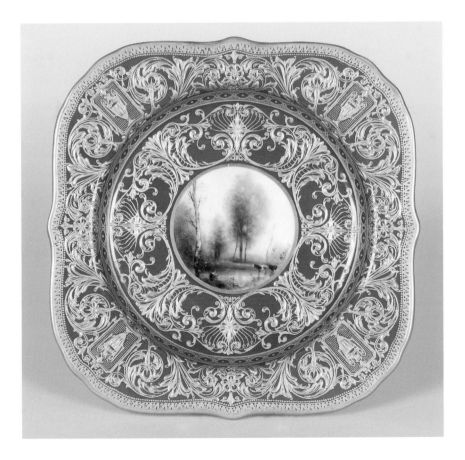

A plate from one of Royal Worcester's Kellogg Services, with lavish raised-paste gilding. The central panel after Corot is by Harry Davis. 21 cm wide, dated 1928.

ever made in the city of Derby. Derby's dinner service involved different painted designs for each course, by the factory's top artists. The raised goldwork on every piece was simply breathtaking. It is hard to contemplate the hours of artistry and craftsmanship that went into every single plate or cup. In 1928 Royal Worcester's Kellogg Services, two fruit sets made for the family of cereal magnates, were just as sumptuous. One set was painted with French-style landscapes by Harry Davis; the other had winter scenes painted by Harry Stinton. Both sets featured raised and tooled gilding on a bright red ground, the most expensive colour to produce. Each plate cost Judge Gary and the Kelloggs a king's ransom. Long since sold and split up between collectors around the world, pieces occasionally come onto the market today. They are expensive, yes, but allowing for inflation, in real terms they realise a fraction of the price they cost to make in 1909 and 1928, or indeed what such workmanship would cost if it was attempted today.

The artists who signed their names on the Gary and Kellogg sets belonged to teams of highly talented china painters employed by Britain's leading porcelain factories, Royal Doulton, Royal Crown Derby and above all, Royal Worcester. Their fine hand painting was part of a long tradition of masters teaching apprentices, for the craft of china painting takes many years to learn and perfect. To create an impressionistic scene of the Highlands on a Royal Worcester vase, John Stinton mixed his metallic oxide-based colours with a special sticky oil. He knew how the different pigments would perform and change colour and texture during the kiln firing, for he had learnt china painting from his father, who had learnt from his father before him, at Graingers and at Flights china factories in Worcester. John Stinton then taught his own son Harry during a long, seven-year apprenticeship.

A Royal Worcester dish painted with Highland cattle by John Stinton, 28.2 cm wide, dated 1926. The artist has used the dish as a canvas to create his impressionistic scene, an incredible achievement in view of the difficult process of china painting.

LEFT
*Royal Worcester plates
painted by Harry Davis
with London scenes,
14 cm in diameter, dated
1926. In 1920 Harry
Davis visited London
for a week and made
sketches. His work
perfectly captured the
atmosphere and
excitement of London
in the smog.*

BELOW
*A Royal Crown Derby
vase by Désiré Leroy,
21 cm high, dated 1896.
Leroy was one of the last
all-round 'decorators', for
he painted the bird panel
and also added the raised
gilding and jewelled
backgrounds.*

The artists at Royal Worcester each had their own specialist subject. John and Harry Stinton both painted Scottish scenes with Highland cattle. John's brother James painted game birds. Harry Davis, who painted Corot-style French landscapes on the Kellogg Service, was a master at many subjects but more than any other he painted Highland scenes with sheep instead of cattle. Other artists painted birds, or flowers or fruit. All waited until orders arrived for their work. At times during the 1930s work was thin on the ground and without work to do, painters didn't get paid. The senior artists, especially the Stinton family, were kept pretty busy, for there was almost constant demand for their Highland scenes. Their customers included ex-patriot British farmers in Australia or New Zealand who wanted memories of home, nostalgic scenes painted onto Royal Worcester's vases or dainty cups and saucers.

While many of the subjects hand painted on the porcelain at Worcester and at Doultons were traditional, the colouring and atmospheric effects were bright and refreshingly modern. The artists blended their colours in a subtle manner more reminiscent of the French Impressionists than of British china painting in the past. The shapes of the vases were mostly traditional, however; indeed, many of Worcester's had been modelled by James Hadley back in the nineteenth century. Bright gilding and shaded bronze finished off the borders and handles. The overall effect was still old fashioned but this is what the factory's wealthy customers wanted.

Some of the finest artistry was so incredible it is hard to believe it really was made by hand. At Royal Crown Derby Désiré Leroy was one of the last of the great all-round 'decorators'. Not only did he paint incredibly fine flowers, he also did the coloured groundlay and the raised gilding and applied tiny jewels of coloured enamel to finish off his vases. Leroy's work was luxury 'cabinet' porcelain of the very finest quality and was incredibly expensive. Royal Worcester went even further into the realms of disbelief with the craftsmanship of George Owen. Owen was a 'reticulator' who pierced porcelain vases with patterns of tiny holes while the clay was still wet. Using hand and eye alone, row upon perfect row of minute geometric shapes were cut out of the porcelain to create a net of the most incredible precision.

The work of Désiré Leroy and George Owen was bought by connoisseur collectors but early in the twentieth century such wealthy individuals were few and far between. The depression that followed the First World War changed the marketplace totally. Customers wanted 'cheap and cheerful' in every sense. The public demanded affordable tableware that was lively and highly coloured, and in Britain their thirst was quenched by pottery manufacturers. The 'art deco' designs of Clarice Cliff and colourful moulded jugs made by Burleigh pottery were of earthenware, not fine porcelain.

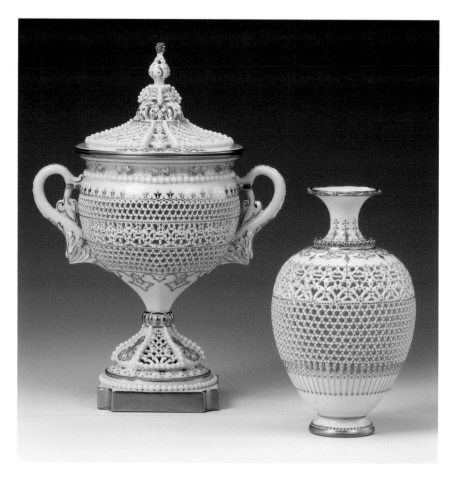

Two Royal Worcester vases by George Owen who pierced his porcelain with the most incredible precision, 20 cm and 13 cm high, with factory marks in gold and date codes for 1911 and 1912.

In Staffordshire in the 1920s, Doultons and the Shelley Pottery made art deco tea sets using fine bone china but the results were generally tame alongside the vibrant patterns of Clarice Cliff. John Wadsworth tried to convince the management at Mintons that art deco was the way forward but he met much resistance. Wadsworth jumped ship and went to Royal Worcester where his suggestions for more modern designs fell on even deafer ears. The china factories were so firmly set in their ways they could not believe their customers wanted something so shockingly new.

One of the few real innovations to be made in British porcelain was Wedgwood's 'Fairyland Lustre'. The creation of Daisy Makeig-Jones, colourful bowls and vases were decorated with scenes from a fantasy world populated by elves, goblins and other fairy-folk. Even in the decadent 1920s many customers found Fairyland a little too disturbing, and from Wedgwood came a more gentle range of lustre wares decorated with fish, butterflies and Chinese dragons. Mintons and Royal Worcester made half-hearted attempts to copy Wedgwood's lustre but their customers didn't respond. Instead Royal Crown Derby kept on making the same Imari patterns, Belleek kept on making shell-shaped tea sets, Mintons still made *pâte-sur-pâte*. Queen Mary had visited the Potteries in 1913 and in its review of the occasion *The Connoisseur* magazine commented on the lack of modern design compared with the Continent of Europe. In the 1930s firms like Paragon China, Coalport and Royal Albert continued to specialise in tea sets that looked and felt Victorian.

After the Second World War so many attitudes changed. The war brought hardships that destroyed the home market for fine porcelain. 'Utility' rules meant only plain,

A Shelley China 'Sunray' pattern tea service using their 'Vogue' shape. Shelley tea sets sum up the spirit of art deco that excited Britain in the 1920s and 1930s.

A Wedgwood bone china lampshade, the traditional dancing figures from the eighteenth century re-issued to cast an eerie glow over a 1920s home. 33.5 cm diameter.

undecorated pottery could be sold in Britain until the early 1950s. Instead, decorated china was made for 'export only'. America and Canada received shipments of traditional tableware that was hardly inspired. Once utility restrictions were lifted, Britain entered a different world. The 1950s was the age of Pyrex and plastic. Materials in the home had to be modern and functional. The public wanted simplicity in design

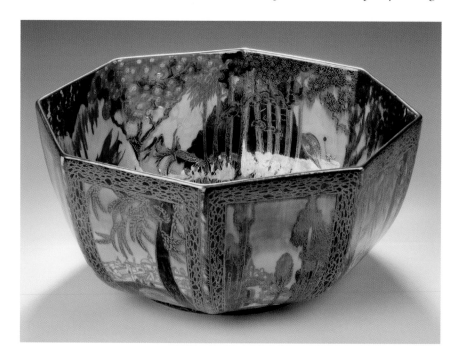

A Wedgwood 'Fairyland Lustre' octagonal bowl decorated with the 'Boxing Match' pattern. 26 cm wide, c. 1930. Daisy Makeig-Jones's designs can be jolly, but many found them disturbing.

and rejected anything traditional. In the Potteries a few earthenware manufacturers such as Midwinter responded with inexpensive new ranges.

The leading porcelain manufacturers in Britain responded with plain tableware patterns but they were not necessarily modern. Coloured border patterns with gold trim satisfied customers in America and Canada, which remained the most important marketplaces. As wedding presents, families bought very expensive dinner services. Many had intricate borders of 'acid gold', a narrow, textured border pattern etched into the glaze and covered with a band of bright gold. Smart and costly, such sets were profitable for the factories, but there were problems ahead. The most popular patterns were timeless and didn't need to be replaced by the next generation. Then along came the dishwasher. In America in the 1950s and '60s, the dishwasher became a status symbol, followed a decade later by the microwave oven. Fine porcelain with gold trim suddenly became the last thing families wanted.

One major response was 'oven to tableware'. In 1970 Royal Worcester opened a new extension to their factory devoted entirely to the mass production of ovenware. Instead of bone china, this was hard paste or true porcelain, fired at a high temperature and able to withstand the heat of an oven during use. This new porcelain was a huge success. Using coloured lithographic prints or 'decals', Royal Worcester's 'Evesham' pattern of fruit and plant sprays became one of the most popular tableware designs used all over the world. Meanwhile the rest of the Worcester factory discovered that a new term had entered porcelain vocabulary. The 1960s and '70s was the era of the 'limited edition'.

A Royal Crown Derby dinner service of the 'St George' pattern with an intricate 'acid gold' border. In post-war Britain the leading china makers sold costly designs like these for export, while pottery manufacturers made more modern and cheaper patterns for the home market.

Chapter Nine

FIGURINES, COLLECTABLES AND LIMITED EDITIONS: 1910–2000

T HE REBIRTH of the porcelain figure in Britain was a curious side effect of the First World War. The Board of Trade encouraged British manufacturers to produce crafts that would compete with products previously imported from Germany. Bombarding the world with English porcelain copies of Dresden figurines sounds like a rather desperate means of undermining the German economy, but the Board of Trade was taken seriously. In 1916, Royal Worcester issued a new series of military figures, single soldiers dressed in historical uniforms. These copied a popular range of historical figures previously made in Dresden. Other Royal Worcester productions during the war were directly inspired by Dresden, including a set of bird models perched awkwardly on stumps. A few ladies and children in crinolines and some curiously attractive nude studies were direct copies of German prototypes, but while figures like these had been popular on the continent, they failed to appeal to Worcester's customers and once the war ended production was mostly abandoned.

Royal Crown Derby and Royal Doulton also created new figure models during the war, but in terms of figure production in Britain, Doultons was already far ahead of the game. The Art Director, Charles Noke, knew a lot about figures for he had worked at Royal Worcester under James Hadley and joined Doultons in 1889 as a senior modeller. Early in the twentieth century Noke worked on developing glazes (see page 86) and he returned to figures in 1912. He produced some new models of his own, but fearing perhaps that his own work might be old-fashioned, Noke bought in some new models from freelance sculptors. Their figure-making department was re-launched publicly in 1913 to coincide with the royal visit by George V and Queen Mary. When the Queen saw a little figure of a boy in a nightgown by a leading London ceramic artist Charles Vyse, she apparently exclaimed, 'What a darling'. Queen Mary ordered several examples of the figure that Doultons re-named 'Darling' in her honour, and this gave the firm's new figure range enormous publicity.

Royal Doulton's answer to the Board of Trade's appeal was a new take on the lace-covered crinoline ladies from Dresden. Too much detail made the Dresden figures expensive. Doultons used clever painting to convey movement and pattern. It looks as though their china ladies wear flowing skirts, the patterns blurred by swirling movement. This is a trick of the artist's brush, for the modelling is actually

OPPOSITE
A Royal Doulton figure of The Sunshine Girl, modelled by Leslie Harradine in 1929, 12.7 cm high. This reflects the Art Deco taste of the time.

97

quite simple. A new team of young lady painters was engaged, for this was wartime and women replaced a large part of the workforces in Staffordshire ceramic factories. They were taught new techniques.

Royal Worcester and Royal Crown Derby returned to their old-fashioned styles after the war and mostly gave up on figure production. Worcester preferred to make James Hadley's nineteenth-century models rather than commission new ones. Thank goodness Royal Doulton saw things differently. Noke modelled some new historical

and theatrical figures which were certainly old fashioned, but he also created a number of curious eastern subjects and the first of many characters from Charles Dickens. More importantly, Noke engaged a new freelance modeller. Leslie Harradine had worked at Doultons making stoneware at Lambeth before the war but had emigrated to Canada as a farmer. Wounded in action in the war, Harradine saw his future differently and set up as a freelance artist in London. Noke remembered his former colleague and commissioned a series of new models suitable for porcelain production. In the 1920s customers wanted china figures that were sweet and sentimental. They also called for subjects that were more frivolous and even exotic. They no longer wanted the ivory and bronze colouring that Worcester still used for their Hadley figures. Noke realised Doultons' new figures would sell better if they were gaily coloured.

Leslie Harradine was incredibly prolific, creating a huge number of different models for Doulton over the next forty years. Some sold better than others, of course, but he was responsible for relatively few failures. Some models were remarkably successful. 'Top o' the Hill' and 'Autumn Breezes' were perhaps the most successful of all. Both show pretty young ladies wearing long dresses that are caught up in a gust of wind. By means of a simple technique of light and shade, Harradine's girls looked as though their dresses were moving. By comparison, the German 'bisque' figures that were aimed at the mass market seemed still and lifeless. Doultons' girls were jovial and free, and still they were affordable.

ABOVE LEFT
A Royal Doulton figure of 'Top o' the Hill', modelled by Leslie Harradine and produced in huge numbers over a period of more than sixty years.

ABOVE
Royal Doulton's figure 'The Jester' by Charles Noke was originally intended to be coloured in vellum and gold in the manner of Hadley's Worcester figures. It was far more successful in the 1920s when re-issued in a variety of different colourways.

Freda Doughty's figures for Royal Worcester depict real children. These are from her most popular series representing the days of the week, produced from the 1930s until the 1990s. Earlier examples were painted with greater care.

The shaded patterns on the young ladies' dresses contrasted with a different style of colouring used on other Doulton figures. Painted blocks of bright colours suited the harlequinade costumes of Charles Noke's model of 'The Jester', while Leslie Harradine's 'Old Balloon Lady' was a brilliant idea. A modelled bunch of balloons was very easy to paint in different primary colours. The Balloon Lady suited traditional homes as well as modern. Tradition was important in Britain and even more so in the Americas and Antipodes. The writings of Charles Dickens were second only to Shakespeare in popularity, conveying images of 'ye olde England' around the globe. The first few figures of Dickens characters sold well and this encouraged Doultons to make more, expanding the set available.

Sets of figures were a brilliant commercial idea. Customers bought one then another and presents for birthdays and Christmas gifts meant that families came back for more. Doultons discovered this with their 'Series Ware', a full range of giftware and tableware with a different image printed on each piece, together forming a series of related subjects. Sets of plates were made, each with a different figure from Shakespeare's plays. Other giftware had the perennially popular Dickens characters. Colour printing kept the price down, and Series Ware was made in earthenware too as a cheaper alternative to porcelain.

Charles Noke is credited with reinventing the Toby Jug. Doultons' 'Character Jugs' followed in the traditions of old Staffordshire pottery Tobies, although they were modelled in the form of just a head and shoulder bust, rather than a full-length figure. Made in earthenware rather than in bone china, the Character Jugs were perfect decoration for pubs or bars, but decorated many homes too. The Doulton jugs led to a great number of imitations.

It took Royal Worcester a while to realise that they had missed a big opportunity. By 1930 Royal Doulton was making a vast range of porcelain figures. Worcester's new managing director, Joe Gimson, knew the factory had to do some serious catching up. Taking a leaf from Charles Noke's book, Gimson travelled to London and met a number of leading freelance modellers, commissioning a wide range of subjects. When these were offered for sale in 1931-2, the public reaction was mixed. Curious art deco animals and stylised figures as bookends were better suited for pottery than fine porcelain and Royal Worcester's customers didn't understand them. On the other hand, Joe Gimson learnt that on the fine porcelain stage it could be all right to perform with children and animals.

Freda Doughty captured the charming innocence of real children. Her figures were simple and full of movement. Their costumes were plain shirts and smock dresses that were easy to colour, so they were not expensive. Royal Worcester also learnt from Doultons that it was important to take care over the painting of the faces. Pretty figures and charming expressions sold well. Also Doulton had shown that sets make sense. Freda Doughty created a set of figures representing the different months of the year and days of the week – perfect Christening presents. Her figures modelled in the 1930s were still selling in large numbers forty years later. They became competition for Royal Doulton lady figures by Leslie Harradine and a new successful modeller, Peggy Davies, who continued the collections of Doulton Ladies.

Doris Lindner was the other most important modeller at Royal Worcester. In 1932 her first small models of dogs sold well and so Joe Gimson asked for a series of inexpensive studies of different breeds of dogs. Doultons had issued a range of different small animal models, similar to ornaments previously made by Royal Copenhagen and various factories in Germany. For Royal Worcester Doris Lindner made all kinds of dogs, foxhounds and foxes, horses, young farm animals and wild animals. Eva Soper made a large set of British garden birds. At Worcester and at Doultons all their animals were carefully coloured. After the Second World War, porcelain animal ornaments proved expensive and firms like Beswick in Staffordshire made cheaper versions in pottery.

The war disrupted production at all British china factories and when manufacture resumed, ornamental porcelain could only be made for

A Royal Doulton figure group curiously modelled by hand by Peggy Davies, 23 cm wide, c. 1950. Peggy Davies continued the traditions of the Doulton Ladies and also took her inspiration from earlier, eighteenth-century china figures.

A pair of 'Redstarts on Gorse' and the 'Chiffchaff on Hogweed', limited editions from the English series of the Doughty Birds. In the 1960s these were ground-breaking creations.

BELOW LEFT
Royal Worcester dog models by Doris Lindner proved to be enormously popular. An extensive set of individual breeds was made in the 1930s.

BELOW RIGHT
Lieutenant Colonel Harry Llewellyn on his horse 'Foxhunter', Doris Lindner's equestrian study, 30.5 cm high, introduced by Royal Worcester in 1960 as a limited edition of five hundred.

export. With the American market in mind, Royal Worcester was working on a set of larger bird studies modelled by Freda Doughty's sister Dorothy. An American art publisher, Alex Dickens, had initially commissioned a set of plates decorated with birds after the famous Audubon prints. These were made as limited editions, and their success led Dickens to order the first 'Doughty Birds' as editions produced in strictly limited numbers.

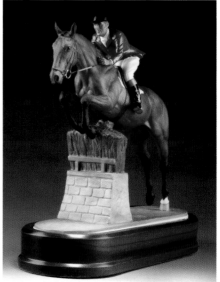

The idea of a limited edition was not a totally new concept, but it became increasingly important in the field of fine china. Only a predetermined number of each Doughty Bird model was made, and when that number had been sold, the moulds were destroyed. Customers knew that their purchase was special and that no more than the set number of models would ever be made. This assurance gave buyers confidence that a costly piece of porcelain was specially crafted, something for a collector and more than just an ornament. In the case of the Doughty Birds, these truly were groundbreaking creations. The porcelain birds were incredibly realistic, using a matt glaze that doesn't look like porcelain at all. They perch on china flowers where every individual petal and stamen was modelled by hand. The potters at Royal Worcester had to devise ingenious methods of removable supports to prevent the birds and flowers collapsing in the kiln. Never before had such complicated porcelain models been cast, assembled and fired in one piece without collapsing.

Worcester was leading the world in modern porcelain sculpture. Doris Lindner was asked to create more ambitious models to be made as limited editions. This started with a statue of Princess Elizabeth on horseback, issued in 1947 in a limited edition of just a hundred copies. A collection of champion cattle followed, along with single models of horses and equestrian groups of show-jumpers and racehorses. Other modellers created further sets of sculptures – historical figures, game birds, tropical fish and ladies in Victorian costumes or nursing uniforms. As limited editions grew in popularity, Royal Worcester resisted the temptation to make more than 500 or in some cases up to 750 individual models. They could have sold many more and in most cases the editions were heavily over-subscribed, shooting up in value on a secondary market.

The Worcester figures and models were all superbly made, but the same cannot be said for all items subsequently issued as limited editions. By the 1970s you could hardly turn a page of a magazine or a newspaper colour-supplement without viewing advertisements for 'collectors' plates'. These were literally manufactured collectables. They used new technology that allowed a colour reproduction of an image or of a painting to be reproduced in fine detail. An artist would paint one image that was photographed. Decals were then made and five hundred, five thousand or fifty thousand copies could be produced at very little cost. Basically you could make as many identical plates as you thought you could sell. The more you made, the bigger the profit.

Responsible manufacturers were careful not to kill the golden goose. Firms like Coalport, Wedgwood and Royal Doulton issued individually numbered certificates with their sets of collectors' plates. Other firms that sold the limited editions issued price guides and indexes showing how the values of certain editions had increased. It wasn't just plates. Sets of coins and stamps and even tea-towels were sold as limited

'Variations on a Geometric Theme', one from a set of six plates created in 1975 by important British artist Eduardo Palozzi and made by Wedgwood in an edition of just two hundred sets. Limited edition collectors' plates were rarely made in such small editions.

A Coalport vase issued in 1980 to commemorate the Queen Mother's 80th birthday. Painted with a scene of Glamis Castle, a limited edition of eighty vases was produced. Many more of the Queen Mother's birthdays were celebrated in porcelain over the next twenty years.

editions. Porcelain makers made figurines, loving cups, vases, goblets and tea sets. Some were very good quality, nicely finished off with gilding, but this wasn't always the case.

It all came to a head in 1977. This was the year of the Silver Jubilee of Queen Elizabeth II. More souvenirs were manufactured than there were people living in Britain. Millions of pieces of porcelain were made, a high percentage as limited editions. Firms like Paragon China had specialised in royal commemoratives since the 1930s and their mugs and loving cups were well designed. Customers who bought such pieces naturally assumed that their pieces would perform like Worcester's limited edition figures and increase dramatically in value. All china makers did well in 1977 and sold vast numbers of Jubilee souvenirs. For the wedding of Charles and Diana in 1981, it was a royal boom time all over again. Even though many customers thought the royal wedding souvenirs were tasteless, even the really tacky ones sold quite well.

The bubble burst when collectors came to try and sell their Jubilee plates and Charles and Di wedding mugs on the secondary market. Everyone who wanted one had bought one at the time. A few really special pieces did hold their value, but most proved to be impossible to sell. People realised that many collectors' plates had been something of a con. They had cost next to nothing to make and indeed many were manufactured in the Far East. The cost of advertising them for sale in magazines had actually been much greater than the cost of making the plates themselves. The plates had cost less than the packaging. Commemoratives were made for the Queen Mother's 80th birthday, then for her 85th, and her 90th. By the time she celebrated her 100th birthday, nobody was interested in items that commemorated her previous birthdays. They ended up in charity shops.

Times had changed. Porcelain manufacturers seriously burnt their fingers with the Millennium celebrations in 2000. Most factories produced more than they could sell and makers faced heavy losses. When the Queen celebrated her Golden Jubilee in 2002, the commemorative industry had learnt its lesson and production was surprisingly low key. This was very bad news for the British porcelain industry that for so many years had relied on souvenirs and limited editions for its livelihood. China figurines were now being made more cheaply in the Far East than ever before and resin was the new wonder material. Factories in the UK could not compete. Fine porcelain tableware has had its day too. The new fashion for minimalism means that the only crockery that sells well today is plain white, and this is made more cheaply in China than in England. After selling their souls in the name of outsourcing, without success, one after the other, great British institutions like Mintons, Royal Doulton, Royal Worcester and Wedgwood have gone into administration.

It is to be hoped that there is a future for porcelain in Britain. At the time of writing workmen at Royal Crown Derby still paint their Imari designs. Belleek craftsmen still weave their baskets from tiny strands of white porcelain. Craftsmen who were once trained at Worcester work for a small porcelain factory in the nearby

Bronté Porcelain makes fine small figurines as candle snuffers. Horatio Nelson and Isambard Kingdom Brunel, introduced in 2005 and 2008, are modelled with great skill combined with historical accuracy.

town of Malvern. Here Bronté Porcelain makes fine small figurines as candle-snuffers, superb models of birds and horses and hand-painted china plaques and cups and saucers. The scale is small, but they have inherited the traditions of James Hadley, Doris Lindner and Harry Stinton. In Lowestoft in Suffolk a new Lowestoft porcelain company makes china in the same way as its eighteenth-century namesake. This will never be as valuable, but at least some porcelain is still made in Britain.

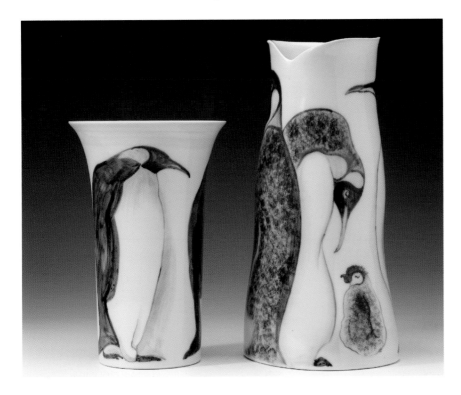

'Penguins', two British porcelain vases by Grahame Clarke, 31.5 cm high, signed with the artist's monogram and dated 2008. Clarke creates modern porcelain using the ancient technique of underglaze blue.

Chapter Ten

COLLECTING
BRITISH PORCELAIN

THERE has never been a better time to start collecting antique porcelain. There are great opportunities in many different areas and to suit every pocket. With a bit of knowledge and a lot of common sense, pitfalls can be avoided and even a modest collection can give a great deal of pleasure. This book tells the story of British porcelain through three centuries but it is of course impossible to collect every kind of porcelain from every era. You simply have to specialise. Your own taste is the most important factor, but price is a serious consideration. It is not possible to collect rare porcelain from the 1750s without a heavy financial investment, but many other areas are certainly affordable.

Most collectors start almost by accident with a piece of porcelain passed down in the family or simply by spotting an item that appeals in an antique shop. Finding out more information about an object can stir an interest and can even lead to an obsession. Doing some homework and background reading about the subject is essential. The Internet is very helpful and can point the way to specialist books on different porcelain factories, although many are frustratingly out of print. Once you have decided on the kind of porcelain you would like to collect, the next step is again helped by the Internet. Records of previous auction results are available and these will give the range of prices you must expect to pay.

The most popular fields for porcelain collecting are individual makers or factories, followed by collecting a single shape. Periods in history and decorative themes are other collected areas. Worcester is the most-collected make of English porcelain, followed by Royal Doulton, with Coalport, New Hall and Derby just behind. Every factory in Staffordshire, from giants like Mintons to little Machin and Co., has its enthusiasts somewhere. If you choose a big factory like Worcester, you need to specialise further as there is too much available otherwise. A small factory can be studied in great depth, but it can become hard to find new and exciting pieces to purchase.

Shapes with obvious collectors' appeal are teapots and plates, although size can be a restrictive consideration if you have a small home. The space needed to make a nice display can soon run out when you accumulate teapots. Little cream jugs or single coffee cups are very much easier shapes to house. Entire tea services from the nineteenth century are remarkably good value and it feels good to keep a whole set intact, but few houses have room for many tea sets.

Porcelain figures or figurines are very widely collected for they have very obvious appeal. Good examples from Chelsea, Bow and Longton Hall are understandably expensive, but it is surprising how reasonably priced most Derby and later Bow

OPPOSITE
A Lowestoft coffee pot, 23 cm high, c. 1770, the crack around the base held in place with an old metal rivet. With modern methods of conservation, this damage can be cleaned and secured almost invisibly.

ABOVE
Collecting eighteenth-century coffee cups is an excellent way to learn about different British porcelain factories. These examples are: (top row, left to right) Lowestoft and Vauxhall; (bottom row) Chaffers Liverpool, Derby and Champions Bristol.

OPPOSITE TOP
Teacups and saucers by Spode and Coalport with different 'Japan' patterns, c. 1815. At around £40 each in 2009, these are remarkable value considering the workmanship involved.

figures are these days. Nineteenth-century Staffordshire porcelain figures cannot easily be attributed to makers and as a result they are inexpensive. Animal models and cottage-shaped pastille burners are seriously undervalued and offer enormous scope. Victorian figures, either in parian or in the bronze and ivory colouring of Royal Worcester, are also neglected. Twentieth-century Royal Doulton and Royal Worcester figures are readily available, the value determined by rarity.

Most people choosing to collect a specific period are drawn to the eighteenth century. Quite a popular challenge is to try to buy an example from every one of the eighteenth-century British china factories. Worcester and Bow are easy of course, but Isleworth and Limehouse will cost a pretty penny. The Regency period from the early nineteenth century is neglected. The finest products from the Worcester factories, Rockingham and Swansea will always be expensive, but Coalport, Ridgway and Davenport cost far less than they used to. The Victorian period has also fallen out of fashion in the twenty-first century. Great pieces of Mintons are costly, but plenty of impressive pieces from a wide range of makers can cost surprisingly little in view of the huge amount of workmanship involved in their creation. The twentieth century saw pottery take over in the field of modern design. Good art nouveau and art deco British porcelain is hard to find and it is worth seeking out stylish pieces by Shelley and Royal Doulton in particular.

There are few types of decoration that are collected by themselves, with one big exception. Blue and white porcelain, especially from the eighteenth century, has widespread appeal. Collectors can mix products from different English factories as well as the Chinese export prototypes that inspired the designs. Learning to tell different makers of blue and white apart can be a rewarding challenge.

One big tip for a neglected area that deserves more recognition is the splendid Regency period porcelain decorated in the 'Japan' or 'Imari' taste. Coalport, Spode and Derby, and many others, made some incredibly lavish patterns and these can look stunning even in a modern home.

It is vital that you choose to collect an area that is comfortably within your budget. It is a mistake to buy inferior or broken examples simply because these are all you can afford. Always buy the best pieces that you can. Collecting has to be fun, but it is far better to splash out and buy a few really good pieces of porcelain rather than a great number of ordinary ones.

Porcelain collectors have very different opinions when it comes to the topic of damage and restoration. Many people will tell you always to avoid buying damaged pieces and this is sensible advice. On the other hand, there are many wonderful pieces available that still have excitement and rarity that more than excuse a bit of damage. Experienced collectors learn to distinguish those pieces that are sufficiently rare and interesting to be worth owning in spite of poor condition.

Attitudes to damage and restoration have changed in recent years. As the rarest early porcelain becomes increasingly difficult to find, broken specimens are certainly better than nothing. Unsightly damage can be concealed by restoration so that, visually, pieces can look as good as new. There are two different kinds of restoration. One sort involves disguising damage totally with colour matching and a surface spray that blends with the porcelain glaze. Top restorers can make a broken piece appear faultless and in certain cases this can be a

BELOW
Often priced below £20, Crested China miniatures by makers such as W. H. Goss are amongst the most affordable of all British porcelain ornaments. These novelty shapes from the First World War include a hand grenade and a search light.

very good thing. Many collectors, though, do not like the feel of porcelain that has been overpainted and sprayed with synthetic glaze. Another school of thought favours 'museum-type' restoration. Chemicals bleach out dirt and cracks so they are hardly noticed at all. Chips and breaks are filled in and colour-matched so that the damage can only be seen on close inspection. Museum repairs can make a damaged piece look ten times better, and still feel like an original and authentic piece of early porcelain.

The cost of restoration is an important consideration. All types of professional restoration – or conservation as some repairers like to call their work – is expensive. It is important to get an estimate and to consider the value of the object before and after restoration. A repaired item can look perfect, but it won't be worth the same as an undamaged piece.

New collectors are increasingly worried about buying a piece of porcelain without realising it has been restored. Modern methods of conservation are very clever and it can take a lot of experience to spot the best restoration. Reputable dealers and auction houses will always tell their customers when they know something they are selling has been restored, but not all sellers are so straightforward and honest. You need to examine any potential purchase very carefully. Look at the danger spots: fingers, hands and necks on porcelain figures, finials and handles on vases and teapots. Above all, always ask the seller if they know of any damage or repair and get a receipt stating the condition. Most dealers and auctioneers are very honest and will give a receipt and guarantee without question. Never trust anyone who says they don't know if a piece they are selling is restored, as this usually means they are lying.

Collectors are naturally worried about buying fakes. Some of the most valuable early English porcelain was itself made as forgeries of Chinese and Japanese porcelain back in the eighteenth century. All manner of fakes have been made ever since and there is hardly a category of British porcelain that has not at some time attracted the attention of a forger. The best-known porcelain faker was the firm of Edmé Samson & Cie of Paris. For more than a hundred years, Samson copied a wide range of English and Welsh porcelains, especially Chelsea and Worcester. Samson made hard paste porcelain that looks very different to British soft paste or bone china, but it is only easy to tell if you have handled enough pieces to learn to tell the difference.

As well as all kinds of outright fakes, an area that tricks more collectors than any other is the subject of redecoration. This is where an authentic piece of old porcelain with simple decoration has been repainted with a far more valuable pattern and re-fired in a kiln at a much later date. This doesn't only affect eighteenth-century porcelain. Many Royal Doulton figures have had rare colour variations added to greatly increase the potential value, while Royal Worcester plates with plain centres have been repainted recently with scenes purporting to be by top artists like the Stintons or Harry Davis.

The only sure way to avoid clever fakes is to learn as much as you can about your subject and handle as many genuine pieces as possible to get a feel for the real thing. As with restoration, you should buy only from reputable dealers and auctioneers and always get a receipt stating the maker, condition and date of manufacture of any purchase.

Fine British porcelain is increasingly sold on the Internet. This provides collectors with a wealth of opportunity but also presents other risks. When buying from an image on your computer screen, you have to rely on the integrity of the sellers and trust they have correctly described an item and listed any repairs or damage. When you view a piece of porcelain in an auction or at an antiques fair, you can gently tap it or ping it to see if it 'rings' – a dull clunk can indicate a fine crack somewhere. Internet sellers often miss minor cracks, as well as more major restoration. Don't be afraid to buy online, just ask the same questions you would ask a dealer or auctioneer face to face and get reassurance before you bid or click the 'buy' button.

As long as you are sensible, collecting British porcelain is easy and fun. There is plenty available to buy and many great museum collections to visit and enjoy. If you want to get further involved you can join other collectors on study weekends or seminars organised by ceramic collectors' societies. Specialist ceramic fairs bring together like-minded dealers and there are plenty of auctions devoted to the best British ceramics. So if this book has inspired you, seize the chance and start collecting. The pleasure of porcelain is infectious.

This 'redecorated' Worcester teapot illustrates the work of a late nineteenth-century forger. The original simple floral sprig pattern was ground away and replaced with desirable figure painting on a fake claret ground. 17 cm high.

INDEX